Electronic Dance Music

Critical Perspectives on Music and Society

Series Editor: David Arditi, University of Texas at Arlington

This book series produces books that present a critical perspective on popular music and the music industry. Two dominant strains of thought exist for the study of popular music. First, many texts in the popular culture tradition celebrate the artists, fans, and cultures that arise from popular music. Second, Music Industry Studies texts give students a "how-to" perspective on making it in the music industry. In both cases, texts rarely address the way that the music industry produces and reproduces power. The purpose of this book series is to provide a platform for authors who explore the social production of music; as such it is broadly interdisciplinary.

The series invites submissions by scholars from the fields of cultural studies, American studies, history, sociology, literature, communication, media studies, music, women's studies, ethnic studies, popular culture, music industry studies, political science, economics, and history.

Specific topics addressed:

Musicians as Labor
Identity (Sex, Gender, Race, Ethnicity, Disability, and Sexuality)
Critical Representations
Music Industry Studies
Music in the Global South
Production of Genres
New/Old Technologies
Sound Studies
Access inequalities to music production and consumption
Spaces of music production, creation, and consumption

Electronic Dance Music: From Deviant Subculture to Culture Industry by Christopher
    T. Conner and David R. Dickens
Code Musicology: From Hardwired to Software by Denis Crowdy
Mixtape Nostalgia: Culture, Memory, and Representation by Jehnie I. Burns
iTake-Over: The Recording Industry in the Streaming Era, Second Edition by
    David Arditi
Cruisicology: The Music Culture of Cruise Ships by David Cashman and Philip Hayward
"This Is America": Race, Gender, and Politics in America's Musical Landscape by
    Katie Rios

Electronic Dance Music

From Deviant Subculture to Culture Industry

Christopher T. Conner and David R. Dickens

LEXINGTON BOOKS

Lanham • Boulder • New York • London

Published by Lexington Books
An imprint of The Rowman & Littlefield Publishing Group, Inc.
4501 Forbes Boulevard, Suite 200, Lanham, Maryland 20706
www.rowman.com

86-90 Paul Street, London EC2A 4NE

British Library Cataloguing in Publication Information Available

Library of Congress Cataloging-in-Publication Data

Names: Conner, Christopher T., 1981- author. | Dickens, David R., author.
Title: Electronic dance music : from deviant subculture to culture industry / Christopher T. Conner and David R. Dickens.
Description: Lanham : Lexington Books, 2023. | Series: Critical perspectives on music and society | Includes bibliographical references and index. | Summary: "This text explores how the Electronic Dance Music subculture transitioned from a marginalized deviant subculture to a billion-dollar culture industry, looking at how the culture's success has undermined in-group solidarity and marginalized those who helped pioneer it"—Provided by publisher.
Identifiers: LCCN 2022060864 (print) | LCCN 2022060865 (ebook) | ISBN 9781793620392 (cloth) | ISBN 9781793620415 (paperback) | ISBN 9781793620408 (ebook)
Subjects: LCSH: Electronic dance music—Social aspects—History. | Rave culture.
Classification: LCC ML3918.U53 C65 2023 (print) | LCC ML3918.U53 (ebook) | DDC 781.648—dc23/eng/20221220
LC record available at https://lccn.loc.gov/2022060864
LC ebook record available at https://lccn.loc.gov/2022060865

Chris would like to dedicate this project to the memory of David R. Dickens—a friend, father, and all-around real mensch.

David would like to dedicate this book to his darling wife, Angelique Dickens.

Contents

Acknowledgments

We would like to thank our friends and colleagues at the University of Nevada, Las Vegas—especially Robert Futrell, Connie Dye, and Pam Weiss. We also want to thank our editor, Courtney Morales, who never stopped encouraging us to complete this project. Danielle Hidalgo, Andi Dassopoulos, and Joan Hermsen also acted as fantastic colleagues helping out with this study. We also received a wide range of financial support from several sources, including the Graduate College at the University of Nevada, Las Vegas, the Sweet Summer Sabbatical, the Knox College Professional Development Fund, and the Department of Sociology at the University of Missouri, Columbia.

There were a variety of people and organizations outside academia that aided to this project in a variety of ways. The images in this text are courtesy of Michael Tullberg, the Rave preservation project, and a variety of unnamed sources. Chris, the first author, was motivated to initiate this study based on his small role in the Indianapolis music scene and wishes to thank Joel Adams, Lynn Albers, Gretchen Banning, Greg Brenner, Caroline Courtney, "Disco Donnie" Estopinol, Jason Gehlhausen, Andrea, Amanda Grube, Kyle Hodges, Slater Hogan, Pierre Jackson, John Larner, Topher Jones, Janine and Ken Jordan, Dorothy Larosa-Fyffe, Kyle Matthews, Jack Shepler, Stephanie Swanson, "Tuffty," Sarah Vain, and many others who gave us access to the world of electronic dance music. Additionally, various livestreamers helped provide hours of breaks while finishing this project—Echoplex Media, Gremloe, Homozygoat, James from the Internet, Polly People, and QAnon Anonymous. Finally, thanks to the workers at all of the coffee shops in Columbia, Missouri.

Introduction

Music subcultures have long occupied the minds of the public and sociologists alike, partly because of their music and style of dress but also because of the alternative lifestyles that many of them propose. While previous music subcultures, like hippie, rock, and punk stood directly in opposition to the dominant culture of their time, the Electronic Dance Music (EDM) subculture resisted the status quo in a variety of different ways. The term EDM refers to a collection of music genres that originated in Chicago and Detroit in the 1980s, heavily influenced by advances in new computing technology (Reynolds 1999, 2012). The EDM subculture was far less active in organizing for overtly political reasons (i.e., protesting), but it excelled at subverting authority by using clandestine venues (i.e., underground nightclubs, warehouses, and other unused urban spaces) in order to bring together a broad variety of marginalized groups to exchange a plethora of ideas. Their style stood in stark contrast to punk, goth, and rock subcultures through their use of bright day-glow colors and a positive playfulness within the culture. However, instead of abandoning the ideas of previous generations that had come before them, they built upon these in order to create something altogether new.

The music itself was developed by musicians who began experimenting with developments in new computer technologies. These musical pioneers came primarily from Chicago, and dubbed their style "House music." As a genre, "house" was melodic in character and consisted of vocals and themes emphasizing sexual and sensuous. However, "house" also offered an escape from mainstream society by advancing alternative normative claims about the way things ought to be. A particularly important point that previous studies of EDM have underplayed is that the music was established by queer men of color, and this may explain many of the themes embedded in the original

1

EDM subculture. Thus, some argue, house music resembled earlier race hymns by calling for listeners to "be free," or to "rise up," and the music itself often contained a quasi-religious element. As such, the genre first took root within a predominately African American and Latinx Gay audience (Silcott 1999).

Not long after the development of house music, musicians in Detroit also began experimenting to create their own genre of music. Also pioneered by queer men of color, Detroit developed a somewhat futuristic and harsher style of EDM dubbed "techno." Techno incorporated guitars, mechanized beats, and computerized sounds (Brewster and Broughton 2000; Silcott 1999). Detroit's harder style has been linked by some to the failing automotive industry in the city. Thus, techno's aggressive style may be seen as a reaction to the social conditions that affected the lives of its creators—providing a critique of contemporary urban life in Detroit (Reynolds 1999; Silcott 1999).

The EDM subculture organized itself around the values of Peace, Love, Unity, and Respect (PLUR)—though this was itself an evolution of Peace, Love, Unity, Movement (PLUM), which we discuss in chapter 1. Within these cultural values one can see elements of the free love movement of the 1960s, and the strategy of using entertainment as a vehicle for expressing their ideas can be traced more recently to the gay rights movement that came out of the late 1960s (Humphreys 1972: 84). Indeed, queer culture has a long history of organizing in clandestine venues and reappropriating spaces to establish a sense of community among its participants. The EDM subculture also drew upon the values of punk culture, especially its DIY aesthetic, anti-establishment and anti-capitalist beliefs, and appropriation of symbols as a resistance strategy (Fox 1987; Haenfler 2004, 2014; Williams 2011; Haenfler, Johnson, and Jones 2012).

The third element crucial for understanding the emergence of EDM—and one that has been largely overlooked by scholars studying the subculture—is the role of new technologies (Bredow 2006; Vitos 2017). EDM emerged in the late 1980s when electronics were starting to become more affordable in consumer households. This would give access to those who lacked the means to purchase musical equipment and making new instruments (i.e., the synthesizer) more readily affordable in lower middle-class households. The other major technological development was, of course the introduction of personal computers and the Internet. Early on in the subculture's development computers were only available to those working at research universities, but they would later become a crucial component for organizing, exchanging music and ideas, and allowing the music to proliferate around the globe and then return to the United States as a more refined product. Europeans added cultural references, like the distinct style which would come to define the subculture, as well as play a necessary role in the creation of new genres that were more easily mass marketed (i.e., Trance).

This present study seeks to place EDM within a larger historical context in order to understand how the subculture went, in relatively short time, from being perceived as a "deviant" subculture to becoming a multi-billion-dollar culture industry. In doing so, we address several important questions unanswered thus far in the sociological literature on music subcultures and social movements. Among those questions remaining are what happens to the subculture as the music becomes more popular—does it cease to exist and do its more recent enthusiasts maintain some semblance of the group's core ideology? Also, how do longtime members feel about these changes, and are they merely passive participants in this process? Equally important, we also analyze the crucial role played by DJs, promoters, and other event organizers as well as law enforcement and other public officials.

SUBCULTURE, SOCIAL MOVEMENT, COUNTERCULTURE, OR "DEVIANT" SUBCULTURE

An important point of clarity for this study concerns how we utilize the terms subculture, counterculture, movement, and deviant subculture. Strictly speaking, the EDM subculture is best described sociologically as a subculture, or even a deviant subculture. However, a comprehensive reading of the literature reveals that the term subculture is perhaps one of the most contested in sociology. Researchers at the University of Chicago were some of the first to utilize the term and applied it to the study of "deviant" youth involved in criminal behavior (Thomas and Znaniecki 1918; Park and Burgess 1925; Palmer 1928). They proposed that, because urban areas were socially disorganized, individuals were not properly socialized (Thomas and Znaniecki 1918; Park and Burgess 1925; Palmer 1928). Thus, initially, the early Chicago school sociologists saw the development of subcultures as a result of the decline of traditional social institutions (i.e., the family, the church, the school,). While the Chicago School has been portrayed as having a narrow approach, they in fact employed a broad range of approaches in their research (see Shaw 1930; Cressey 1932; Sutherland 1937; Bulmer 1984). The central thread running through their work was the notion that contemporary urban life was producing new types of social organizations.

Later on, development of the concept, subculture, drew upon the work of Robert Merton (1949). Merton's theory of anomie, or strain theory, understood deviance as a response stemming from an incongruity between culturally sanctioned goals and the means to achieve them. The frustration that this produced created feelings of anomie or disconnection, which led to the formation of deviant groups, otherwise known as subcultures. In light of this, theorists in the Chicago School concluded that subcultures emerge to alleviate one's inability to achieve success in society through the development of a new status and value system to take the place of more conventional goals (Cloward and Olin 1960; Cohen 1955). Later scholarship emanating from Chicago would expand usage of the term to a variety of groups, including jazz musicians, pool hall hustlers, and others (Becker 1963; Shaw 1966; Polsky 1967).

The focus on subcultures by the Chicago School was subsequently picked up by British cultural studies theorists, who stressed the role of working-class solidarity, and later, identity politics (Turner 1990; Dickens 1994). If the University of Chicago was the center for subculture studies in the United States, the Birmingham School's Center for Contemporary Cultural Studies (CCCS) was the epicenter for the study of subcultures in the United Kingdom. Cultural studies researchers often studied male working-class youth groups that had a distinct, or fantastic, style (such as mods, rockers, teds, and punks). In their analyses, they understood members of these subcultures as trying to exert resistance against hegemonic forces seeking to make them conform (Clarke et al. 1976). Yet, because these groups can never fully exist outside of the dominant parent culture from which they emerge, they often end up recapitulating the same values they oppose. Through their use of style groups such as rockers, teds, and punks allowed members to temporarily resolve contradictions and produce a unique but similar identity (Williams 2011).

Consisting of mostly cultural critics and literary theorists, the Birmingham School was an interdisciplinary program drawing upon Marx when interpreting subcultures, while applying a micro-level interpretive-based study of the participants. The result of the Birmingham School's approach was the ability to address both the everyday lived reality of subculture members, as well as the structural components of society (Willis 1977; Dickens 1994; Williams 2011). Thus, the power of the Birmingham school lies in analyzing the meanings that individuals produce, and connecting them to larger social structures (Dickens 1994).

Some have criticized the Birmingham School for being overly deterministic and too focused on class as the basis for participation in the subculture. Such criticisms are not fully justified, as the best examples of their work (especially Willis 1977) take into account both social structure and socially constructed meaning (see Dickens 1994). Willis uses the term "counterculture" instead of subculture because he is wary of the cultural relativism the term subculture implies (Willis 1977: xlvi). The problem may be due to the fact that the early members of the Birmingham School were not sociologists. They have also been criticized for not taking gender, sexual orientation, and to a lesser degree, race into consideration (though much of the work from the Birmingham School focused on race, especially that of Stuart Hall, Dick Hebdige, and Paul Gilroy).

Some scholars have argued by using the term "subculture," we are inevitably linking it with the concept of "deviance." In so doing, so they argue, it marginalizes and treats those within it as abnormal (Liazos 1972; Kitsuse 1975). They also argue that this framework allows sociologists to impute their own values to the groups they study (Mills 1943). However, proponents of this framework argue that their work helps in humanizing groups so marginalized (Becker 1963, 1967). Indeed much of the work on LGBTQIA culture, sociology of race and identity, and a variety of other areas draw upon this framework in their analysis of social life.

A second criticism that has been raised against the term "subculture" is that it lacks analytical usefulness because it has been overutilized (see Yinger 1960; Fine and Kleinman 1979). To resolve this concern, some theorists have argued for the development of the term "contraculture" or "counterculture," to differentiate between groups who actively resist the values of the dominant culture and those who do not (Yinger 1960). The argument here is that the term "subculture" implies labeling from the outside, whereas "contraculture" or "counterculture" implies active resistance on the part of the group members themselves. Despite this criticism, recent developments by Hodkinson (2002), Gelder (2007), and Williams (2011) have revitalized the term, arguing for its continued utility.

Contemporary scholars have responded to these criticisms in one of two ways. Some scholars have expanded upon this critique by proposing a post-subculturalist approach. Post-subculturalists draw on the work of Andy Bennett (1999) who criticizes the term for being overly static. In practice, he argues what sociologists call subcultures are in reality temporary and fleeting social forms of organization. He proposes that researchers instead utilize Maffesoli's (1996) concept of neo-tribe as an alternative framework, as it provides a more fluid approach to the study of youth groups. In a similar fashion, Muggleton (2000) argues that social scientists have imputed the meaning where none actually existed in the first place. The post-subculture critique has been highly influential among some EDM scholars in Europe, especially among the early studies on the topic.

EDM scholars using a post-subculture framework exhibit postmodern emphases on fragmentation, decay, and the apolitical nature of social contemporary youth subcultures (see McRobbie 1994; Thornton 1996; Malbon 1999; Reynolds 1999; Bennett 2000, 2001). They instead focus on the hedonistic, fantastic, and consumer orientation of the EDM subculture— echoing earlier concerns of the group as deviant subcultures (see Redhead 1993; Williams 2011), or taking a cultural populist approach (see McGuigan 1992). Instead of seeing youth cultures (especially EDM cultures) as part of an interconnected group, they see a plethora of subcultures based on particular genres within EDM (house, deep house, tech house, techno, dubstep, trance, psytrance, Goa trance, etc.) (Redhead 1993; Bennett 1999; Malbon 1999; Muggleton 2000). Furthermore, post-subculturalists argue, categorizing youth according to their consumption habits and imputing meaning to the group is erroneous.

Others argue that there used to be a coherent EDM subculture, but that it no longer exists and has been absorbed into the more generic notion of club cultures (see Thornton 1996; Hodkinson 2002; Siokou and Moore 2008; Anderson 2009a). What the scholarship of the 1960s saw as important elements in the study of subcultures, post-subculturalists see as limitations. In particular, they point to the EDM subculture's lack of clearly defined group beliefs and attitudes, the diversity of participants, and a focus on hedonistic consumption lacking deeper meaning or substance as reasons for creating a theoretical break from the previous ways youth cultures have been studied (see Redhead 1993; Bennett 1999; Malbon 1999; Muggleton 2000). While the observation that EDM culture has been absorbed into a more general "club culture" in some ways fits the historical narrative of EDM's development offered in this study, what is missing in these accounts is any sort of empirical analysis of how EDM culture was transformed. Interestingly, outside of Gottschalk's (1993) attempt to empirically investigate whether youth exhibit postmodern tendencies, there have been few researchers who actually ask people they are theorizing about what they think. Indeed, Gottschalk's study may yield a much more viable solution to this theoretical debate.

Against the post-subculturalist turn are those who emphasize the more traditional ways that subcultures have been studied. Namely, they place the emphasis on the elements of authenticity, identity, and resistance (Blackman 2007; Fox 1987; Epstein 1994; Haenfler 2004). Instead of claiming that the subculture concept is no longer relevant, they recommend focusing on a variety of analytically distinct dimensions for conceptualizing subcultures including: a distinct style in either dress, music, ritual, and argot (see Cohen 1972), framing one's activity as resistance (however loosely defined), distinct spaces in which members can gather (even if they are translocal or virtual—see Bennett and Peterson 2004), societal reaction that marginalizes or sensationalizes the group, and a shared identity (Hodkinson 2002; Williams 2007; Haenfler 2014).

Scholars of EDM have had to fit their work in between these two arguments. Anderson (2009a), for example, deals with the post-subculturalist critique by placing EDM events along a continuum, ranging from authentic raves to commercialized rave-like events. According to Anderson (2009a), the authentic EDM or rave culture of the late 90s no longer exists due to a variety of forces, including commodification of the EDM subculture. She traces the current commercialized form of the EDM subculture to what her interviewees claim is its more authentic past, allowing her to circumvent criticism from post-subculturalists and treat her object of study as an ongoing historical achievement. Moreover, she is able to analyze how this change occurred by examining the larger structural forces alongside participants' interaction in the setting. Similarly, Hidalgo (2014, 2022) builds upon Anderson's work by showing how authenticity is incorporated into complex branding and marketing strategies. As Hidalgo argues, authenticity and commercialization are linked and at times work tangentially, while at other times one is sacrificed in the name of the other. However, we will argue here that, historically, the tradeoff has been more one-directional, with authenticity being sacrificed for profitability.

We acknowledge the criticisms of the post-subculture framework and other definitional criticisms of the term subculture. However, as we hope to show, empirically, the lines between subculture and social movement are blurry. There are times in which the EDM subculture is best described as a social movement, especially in the early formative years. However, as time progressed, the subgroup took on an apolitical stance on social issues and focused almost exclusively on more hedonistic aspects. As we found in interviews with participants, they themselves often used these terms interchangeably. Our usage here reflects our participants' views of themselves. While we sometimes use the term "deviant" before the word subculture, this is done to denote how outsiders reacted, responded, and portrayed the subculture and should not be taken to be a value judgment on our part (see Becker 1963, 1967).

THE PRESENT STUDY

We utilized a mixed qualitative methodological approach in conducting this research study. Since 2015 we have been conducting interviews (both formal and informal) with EDM participants and industry professionals (including booking agents, radio show hosts, DJs, writers, non-profit organizers, and event promoters). Our interview sample consisted of 50 industry insiders (10 women, 40 men), who were responsible for the organization of EDM events—including promoters, DJs, booking agents, nightclub managers, and others involved in the production of EDM. We also interviewed nearly 100 fans of the subculture recruited from personal networks, those we met during our fieldwork, and those we found online forums devoted to EDM. There have been several studies within sociology on the EDM subculture but these these have been partial or incomplete, focusing on the fan experience and largely neglecting the role of producers—though Hidalgo's (2022) work is an exception. Moreover, outside of a handful of scholars (St. John 2004;

Anderson 2009a, 2009b; Hidalgo 2022), few studies have focused on the economic and political structural forces shaping the movement. Prior to 2009, the EDM subculture seemed to be disappearing or in decline (Bennett 1999; Anderson 2009a). However, after that, a shift occurred in the United States which catapulted the EDM subculture into a multi-billion-dollar industry. This study, then, represents an attempt to bridge the gap between Anderson's (2007, 2009a) work and Hidalgo's (2014; 2022) work by answering how this massive shift transpired.

Another important element that differentiates this study from others is the role of the first author. Between 2002 and 2010 he was a music promoter in Indianapolis, and worked with a variety of artists, agents, and other industry professionals. In sociological parlance, he was a complete insider (Adler and Adler 1987). Moreover, as an openly gay male, he was aware of the history of the culture. While some social scientists have criticized insider research as being potentially biased, as others have noted (see Hodkinson 2002) this can also aid researchers in their fields of study. In this case, it came in the way of building a rapport, knowing which questions to ask (and how to ask them), and having insider knowledge that helped frame the research. Toward the end of this study, however, as his length of time outside of the business grew, it proved to be much less of an asset as many simply forgot who he was.

THE CULTURE INDUSTRY

One of the important theoretical concepts that this study addresses is the concept of the "culture industry." As a theoretical concept, the culture industry was first developed in the 1940s in the work of Frankfurt School critical theorists, Max Horkheimer and Theodor Adorno (1972 [1944]). In the introduction to a later article, Adorno (1975 [1967]) points out that the term was developed as a critical response to the notion of "popular culture," which implies that culture emerges spontaneously from the people. Instead, the culture industry concept argues that culture is becoming increasingly imposed in a top-down or administered manner. However, Horkheimer and Adorno's contemporaries understood that authentically produced culture could be co-opted (Schlemback 2015). As we found, this is precisely what happened in the second phase of EDM's development.

The term "culture industry" consists of two main features: standardization and pseudo-individualization. Standardization, Horkheimer and Adorno argued, was made possible by new technologies of mass communication (in their time, the TV, radio, and film). These developments in turn allowed for the application of Fordist-style production techniques that made possible the quick, cheap, and profitable reproduction of cultural commodities. Thus, a sphere of life where economic factors were once relatively minimal is now shaped by them as a primary motivation. The result, according to Horkheimer and Adorno, is a cultural sphere devoid of critical thought and ideologically harmful to consumers by dulling their intellectual capacity. The second feature of the culture industry, pseudo-individualization, refers to the notion that individual cultural products, be they works of art, music, literature, or film, are marketed as unique, when in fact, they are all derived from a common formula.

Adorno and the other Frankfurt School theorists, especially Herbert Marcuse, recognized that there always was a commodified aspect to culture, but with the rise of the culture industry, culture becomes commodified through and through. In a later essay, Adorno explains:

> Ever since these cultural forms first began to earn a living for their creators as commodities in the market place, they had already possessed something of this quality [profit motive]. But then they sought after profit only indirectly, over and above their autonomous essence. New on the part of the culture industry is the direct and undisguised primacy of a precisely and thoroughly calculated efficacy in its most typical products. (1975 [1967]: 13)

This is not to say that communal and political elements have completely disappeared, but rather that they have been extremely marginalized by the corporate profit-oriented nature of the culture industry.

Though Adorno was the most negative critic of the culture industry among the Frankfurt School theorists, even in his later work recognized that culture can never be fully commodified (or rationalized in Weber's sense). Instead, it merely colonizes indigenous or spontaneous forms of culture (see also Frank 1997), as attempts by industry professionals to create cultural products from scratch are often unsuccessful. In a later essay titled "Free Time," Adorno (1991 [1977]) cited a German study in which Dutch citizens actually rejected the mass-mediated messages to which they were exposed. From this, Adorno concluded that the culture industry can never fully erase the critical potential that it promises but does not deliver. This is also pointed out by Paul Piccone (1978) and Slavoj Zizek (1997), who argue that the system even today incorporates a depoliticized concept of dissent or rebellion. Under the logic of capitalism, difference is repackaged through identity politics and then sold back to us (Schlemback 2015).

ORGANIZATION OF THIS BOOK

We conceptualize the EDM subcultures' development in terms of three overlapping phases. Chapter 1 (Phase 1: Beginnings [1980s–1995]), explores the origins of EDM and its early, formative years of development. Here we describe participants' commitment to the subculture's core values of PLUR, and the different threads of inspiration (musical and non-musical) that helped create them. While the precise origins of EDM are a matter of debate, the overall narrative concerning the nature of EDM tends to be the same: technological advances in communications and computing technologies allowed musicians, first in Chicago and later in Detroit, to experiment with new ways of producing music. The Chicago EDM scene developed house music within underground disco clubs frequented by gay Latinx and African Americans (Brewster and Broughton 1999; Silcott 1999; Hindmarch 2001; Lawrence 2016; Madden 2016). Knowledge of their existence often occurred through word of mouth alone (Ramos 2003). The name house itself was a reference to one of these underground clubs, named "The Warehouse."

EDM culture then was both an escape through pleasure and a social commentary on the current state of society (both in the UK and the US). Thus, EDM was grounded in both hedonism and celebration on the one hand, and social critique (of deindustrialization, failing urban economies, class, racial, gender, and sexual inequalities, and rejection of conservative politics) on the other (Brewster and Broughton 2000). EDM enthusiasts practiced these ideals by emphasizing hedonism via dance parties occurring late at night, drinking and taking drugs, breaking copyright through the appropriation of others' music, holding unlicensed parties, holding events in spaces without permission, and generally circumventing the "legitimate" ways of organizing in society.

The organization of EDM events themselves also challenged the notions of genre, form, and expectations through the use of elaborate visuals (lasers, lights, new projection technology, psychedelic imagery, etc.), a pastiche style of dress by participants, the use of non-traditional spaces for events, and the informal dissemination of event locations. While EDM participants did not engage in direct political activism like the hippies or punks before them, they became more political because of the way in which the society reacted to them. Thus, the EDM subculture was about more than just music. It was a response of those who felt real suffering due to their marginalized status, making EDM events a temporary escape (for a more detailed account, see Buckland 2002).

In chapter 2 (Phase II: The Rise of the Rave Outlaw (1995–2009)) we describe the process whereby EDM transitioned into a small, urban youth phenomenon. Key to this transition was increased coverage by mainstream media outlets. This reporting often emphasized hedonistic elements and connected attendance with drug use; however, it also served to popularize the subculture. Sensationalized reporting from a variety of outlets gave public officials the ammunition they needed to marginalize, criminalize, and ultimately outlaw the early EDM subculture. A similar phenomenon also occurred in the UK (see Reynolds 1999; Goode 2004; Peretti 2006). The height of involvement by public officials occurred in 2003 when the then Senator Joseph Biden introduced a legislative bill that effectively criminalized rave events altogether (see Appendix A). The Reducing Americans Vulnerability to Ecstasy (RAVE) Act painted EDM organizers as facilitators of all-night drug parties and criminalized them under expanded crack house laws. Despite an ultimately successful campaign against the bill by rave promoter James D. Estopinal, Jr. (better known to participants as "Disco Donnie"), things would never be the same for the EDM subculture. Certain items (pacifiers, glowsticks, Vick's VapoRub) were outlawed, alongside harm-reduction techniques utilized by many promoters (Sein 2004; Ahrens 2013; Anderson 2009a, 2009b). While these restrictions have lessened over the years, many of these items are still today banned at larger EDM events (Herman 2012). The other important change to occur during this phase was that promoters began to utilize licensed venues as a way to sidestep scrutiny from law enforcement. In so doing, they laid the foundations for the third final phase, which we call in chapter 3, the Culture Industry phase (from 2010 to the present).

During the Culture Industry phase, from approximately 2010 to present, the subculture became a multi-billion-dollar industry, fully integrated into local economies. To provide some context, EDM events such as The Electric Daisy Carnival, the yearly event held in Las Vegas, generated $207 million in taxable revenue and created 618 full-time equivalent jobs in 2012. On a national level, EDM promotion companies such as SFX Entertainment, have become large-scale corporate enterprises. On October 9, 2013, SFX became a publicly traded company and has spent close to $1 billion acquiring other domestic and foreign companies. In this chapter, we analyze how this transition has been made possible and what problems it poses for the members of the subculture. We argue that while earlier decisions were made on artistic principles, today, decisions are made based on profitability (Lloyd 2006; Masquelier 2013; St. John 2009, 2004). Thus, as we explore, success for EDM came at the expense of the core values of the subculture with more political notions of resistance and social change having been undermined altogether.

Chapter 1

Phase I: Beginnings (1980s–1995)

The electronic dance music (EDM) subculture was born out of the underground "house music" disco club scene.[1] Early house music venues were frequented by gay Latinx and African Americans[2] in the late 1980s up until the early 1990s (Brewster and Broughton 1999; Silcott 1999; Hindmarch 2001; Lawrence 2016; Wiltsher 2016). Getting into these underground clubs often required membership, which was obtained by securing a sponsor who was already a member. Thus, entrance to these clandestine venues, and knowledge of their existence, was spread mostly through word of mouth (Brewster and Broughton 1999; Maestro 2003). The name "house" was used to describe a variety of music played at the then-famous Chicago nightclub, "The Warehouse" (located at 206 South Jefferson Street).[3] House music was characterized as soulful due to its roots in disco and the use of strong, often African American, female vocals. House music anthems such as "Move Your Body," "Love Can't Turn Around," and "Sensation" contained strong sexual overtones, while other songs offered escape by urging revelers to be free, rise up, or to keep on moving. Together these themes gave house music a quasi-religious element, in effect resembling spiritual hymns. Not surprisingly, these themes resonated well with listeners, who were themselves marginalized outside of the underground club scene due to their race and sexual orientation (Thomas 1995; Silcott 1999; Hindmarch 2001; Madden 2016).

As a new form of music, house's creators utilized advances in new computing technologies that were just becoming available at the time, along with a fundamentally different way of thinking about performing music. DJs were known for creating seamless performances of sound, going from one song to another without stopping. They were also becoming a staple within the hip-hop scene. One of the distinguishing characteristics of the early house scene was its creators' ability to incorporate different styles into the genre, blending them, and creating something new. A DJ then was a postmodern architecture of sound, splicing together different sounds in order to create something new—similar to postmodern film and painting techniques which utilized pastiche and montage, and challenged traditional notions of genre (Denzin 1994). One of the ways that they challenged traditional notions of music was in how EDM was performed. Performances by some of the early pioneers of EDM music were known for their ability to "mix" different sounds and perform for as long as eight hours or more.

To create their seamless musical performances, early EDM DJs had to splice together tape or manipulate consumer turntables not originally designed for what they were doing (professional turntables would come much later). Some of the early EDM DJs that we spoke with talked about the important development of the drum machine. Drum machines are programmable electronic machines that produced repetitive beats, and these helped DJs match different songs together. They could also be used to insert new musical ideas not in the original song—such as when a DJ remixes a much older song and places a new, more modern melody on top of it. While many DJs today would find this an extremely crude way of performing, or creating music, in these formative years being innovative was more than just an inconvenience—it was a necessity. In many cases DJs would often stumble onto these technological innovations, recognizing how they could be used in ways for which they were not designed, or would create what they needed for their performances. One might argue that the DIY ethic that ran through the 1960s counterculture and the punk rock scene can be observed within these formative years of EDM.

Initially, there was little distinction between those who produced music (producers) and those who performed it (performing DJs). They formed a reciprocal relationship, with the producers making new music, and live DJs performing at clubs introducing it. This closeness between the two was likely the result of early EDMs anti-consumerist stance that was part of the culture. Among producers, there were those creating original music and those who were remix artists. Remix artists were music producers who took music from other artists and added new sounds on top of them. The result is much like how some bands may reinterpret a classic song; however, in some cases, it produces a completely new result—or in some cases, musical odysseys mixing songs from two different music genres. EDM musicians and the culture they helped create were forward-thinking early adapters of emerging advances in technology. This enthusiasm for technology was embedded within the culture which thought that technology could, in some way, solve the problems of society. This is also a notion reflected within the emerging sociological studies of internet culture at the time (Rushkoff 1994; Beran 2019).

While house music was being developed in Chicago, Queer[4] African American men in Detroit were also developing their own harsher-sounding version of EDM. Their sound would come to be known as techno. While house music was primarily concerned with mixing and remixing, and creating melodic sounds, techno was much more centered on producing a new form of music that was much more discordant than Chicago-based house music (Brewster and Broughton 1999; Silcott 1999). The pioneers of techno, again largely Black or Latinx and Queer, established themselves on different philosophical footing. Early pioneers of techno understood that music was an art form and a platform upon which they could criticize society. They drew upon musical influences like Kraftwerk, Depeche Mode, Front 242, and other artists who challenged pop music's racial boundaries. However, they also drew upon Afro-futurism of musicians like Parliament Funkadelic, Stevie Wonder, and others who challenged genre and form using electronic innovation. It thus reflected the social conditions of Detroit, which was witnessing the collapse and exodus of its economic core as a major site of car manufacturing, though its harshness also was a societal critique of these social conditions, including white flight and the aftermath of the collapse of corporate infrastructure (Bredow 2006). The name techno itself also reflects techno's reliance on postmodern thought, as pointed out by some EDM scholars, such as Matos (2015). He notes that the names of groups like Cybertron (an early techno band formed by Rik Davis and Juan Atkins) are a "Tofflerian word splice, combining 'cyborg' and 'cyclotron'" (Matos 2015: 8). Simon Reynolds (1999), one of the first EDM music historians, has also noted the influence of postmodern fiction within techno, and how artists intentionally embedded these themes within their work.

EARLY DEVELOPMENTS

As house and techno music began to mature, DJs from Chicago and Detroit started to make appearances across Europe. One particular hot spot for DJs was Ibiza, a Mediterranean island off Spain's coast, was known for showcasing the latest trends in music. As such, it was popular among tourists. Just like American blues and rock musicians before them, early EDM DJs were imported to Ibiza and across Britain, where they found an audience hungry for this new form of music. While EDM had yet to become popular in the United States, in Europe the sound was met with open arms. As American DJs mixed with Europeans, a cross-pollination of ideas occurred both musically and culturally. Europeans picked up on these developments and began producing their own version of house, called acid house (Collin 2009). Those we talked to described acid house as "a more melodic techno, a blending of house and techno, kind of like the rock music of EDM at the time" (Female DJ 40).

Acid house was initially developed by musicians in the city of Manchester in the United Kingdom and was popular in the late 1980s and early 1990s. The UK's role was so influential that it resulted in a major motion-picture release, "24 Hour Party People" (Winterbottom 2002). As the film shows, the UK added influences from rock and roll, new wave, punk rock, and psychedelic rock. An important point the film makes, is that one can trace a line from subcultures of an earlier era (i.e., mods, rockers, punks, and hippies) to this new emerging EDM subculture. Its arrival in Manchester marked the further fusing together of separate lines of culture into a unique subculture, as one prominent US promoter explained in an in-depth interview:

> Basically, the music came from here. . . . Detroit and Chicago and got big and blew up in Europe. They added the culture, and social scene to it. Then in the 90s, when it came back to the U.S., it was more a social scene. When it came back over, hip-hop was big, so it wasn't cool to be a raver. In the 90s, all the cool people went to these [EDM] parties . . . gay people, transvestites, black people, green people, etc. Everybody in one room, like a hundred people. To me, I'm like holy shit, this massive world you walk into. Everybody was so nice and open. There was no internet too [at least not like today]. . . . I liked dance music but it wasn't solely because of the music. It was more due to the social aspects of it. (Male, 45, Promoter)

The crossover to Europe also brought with it developments in fashion, language, and a shared sense of style and identity—all of which are sociologically important elements of a subculture. The particular style of dress, brought over from Europe, included baggy, loose-fitting, bright, neon-colored clothing, much of which resembled that of the hippie counterculture (Reynolds 1999), though, some scholars note that these styles were also present in the United States through its connections to R&B and hip-hop culture. Despite these diverse origins, both emphasized a rejection of "conventional" (read adult) values in favor of reclaiming of one's youth and an emphasis on notions of playfulness.[5]

The emerging subculture surrounding EDM positioned itself against the established social order. While mainstream culture emphasized hardwork, material success, and being serious, the rave subculture stressed being playful, letting go of inhibitions and responsibilities, and an appreciation for the sensuous (Reynolds 1999; McCall 2001). More specifically, the EDM subculture challenged the system by emphasizing hedonism via dance parties occurring late at night, using illicit substances[6], breaking copyright laws through the sampling of others' music, holding unlicensed parties, holding events in spaces without permission, and generally circumventing conventional "respected" channels of society. This led to the perception by outsiders that those involved in EDM were members of a deviant subculture.

Subcultures and countercultures always emerge in reaction to larger historical and structural contexts (Hebdige 1979). In the case of the EDM subculture, these included the AIDS crisis of the 1980s, the end of the Cold War, the first Gulf War, the LA Riots, and a series of natural disasters, such as Hurricane Andrew in 1992, massive flooding of the Mississippi River in 1993, and a 1993 eastern seaboard blizzard. The EDM subculture also emerged in the shadow of a politically conservative era: the Thatcher and the Reagan administrations' war on drugs, deregulation, the cutting of public funding, a rising national deficit, and an aggressive foreign policy. In the wake of these larger historical forces, the early members we talked to described their general feelings of rejection and isolation, what sociologist Emile Durkheim termed "anomie." They recalled that the EDM subculture gave them a place where they could develop a sense of self, or in their own words, "a place where 'freaks can be freaks'" (Female, 45, DJ). As one self-labeled historian of the scene recalled:

> If you were different in that time [1990–1995], you didn't really have a place you could go. The reason the culture took off was because we gave others a home. We didn't have legitimate venues, and most club owners saw us as weirdos, so we had to create our own spaces. (Male, 39, Fan)

Early EDM culture was about finding an escape through pleasure, combined with a social commentary on the current state of society (both in the UK and the US). Through establishing the EDM subculture members rejected the values of their parent culture, expressed a collective longing for relief (brought on by the social strains mentioned above), and sometimes demonstrated active resistance by collectively organizing (Wilson 2006). Some music critics have also pointed out the countercultural underpinnings of the EDM subculture as being grounded in the twin influences of the sensual (house), and the critical (techno) (see Brewster and Broughton 1999; Reynolds 1999).

A third major development in the culture that shaped the development of EDM was the nostalgia for the counterculture movement of the 1960s. One important figure was Frazier Clark, who produced one of the first underground EDM CD compilations of European EDM titled, "Shamanarchy in The U.K." This new sound came to be known as Acid House, and was a harsher blend of house music and techno—a sound which some claim was intentionally designed to augment the influences of the drug Ecstasy (Vitos 2017). The liner notes of Clark's compilation might best be described as a manifesto. In it he calls upon "unpaid gurilla-rave networks of mad jihad dance fanatics" to use whatever method they could to subvert law-enforcement agencies. In his own words:

> government agencies spending millions of taxpayers money to stamp out unli-
> censed dancing and get everybody back into the pubs before the anarchic spirit
> of dancing with fellow beings under open skies in tangy pagan groves sends
> them barefoot mad and unemployable—as well as unemployed—and living in
> cardboard boxes as many of them already are.
>
> When we start asking why they do it, we come face to face with deeper ques-
> tions like: Can anyone 'own' land, especially 'common land'? What the Hell
> has become of the noble Albion dream of a golden flowering of civilization
> which still lurks in each of our hearts? What went wrong? And what more can
> I do?
>
> Since the '80s, Hippies in the underground have been saying that the only
> hope for the dog-eat-dog Western culture before it destroyed itself and the
> planet was an invention that would enable every single individual in it, one by
> one, to escape the materialist made dream in their heads by getting back in touch
> with their hearts and bodies. . . . You can't have a perfect club in an imperfect
> society: You have to change society. And that's when the wild shamanic energy
> of Rave gets radicalized by meeting Hippy/Punk and comes of age just in time
> to transform the culture. . . . House is different [from other music genres], we
> all feel that. This time, we won't be fooled—we don't have time! If Rock 'n
> Roll was the rebellious trumpet that blew down the walls and left the New City
> of Albion open to us, the people, House is the background music in our head-
> phones, synthesizing the triumphantly shining shamanarchic new rave culture as
> people power re-enters to inherit and assume command (Clark 1992).

Clark's manifesto reflects the ways in which British influences were changing both the musical form and establishing a more clearly defined subculture. At an invited talk in 1996 held at Stanford University, Clark echoed the senti-ments of his manifesto, arguing that a clear line could be drawn from the 1960s hippie counterculture to the more contemporary EDM subculture—the participants he referred to as "Zippies." Coining the term in 1988 (Collin 2009) the term "Zippie," like much of the EDM subculture, was also a word splice between Hippie and Zen Buddhism—meant to accentuate the balance between technology and nature, consumption and spirituality, individuals and community, and anti-capitalism.

Reading Clark's manifesto, one can see the foundations of a countercul-ture offering a radical critique of society—anti-consumerist, anti-capitalist, anti-war, and concern for environmental issues. Thus, in questioning the ownership of music, culture, and ideas, EDM culture was a protest against the social structure of society. However, Clark's manifesto, and his subsequent talk at Stanford, notes the orientation toward building a community bound together by forces other than economic ones and a commitment to social change. However, his manifesto also admonishes the subcultures that had come before it for focusing exclusively on nihilism, apathy, and cynicism without offering an alternative. Clark felt EDM offered both a critique of dominant ideologies, while also providing a competitive alternative that was more positively oriented. In short, Clark was trying to establish something that he felt could change the world.

While Clark has been characterized as an eccentric, others within the scene have also commented on the connection between the EDM subculture and previous subcultures. As one blog poster noted:

> Other generations have all the luck. Their subcultural miscreants were usually tied to some sort of ideological principles. You know, peace, free love, that sort of thing. It's almost as if the preceding counter-cultural movements took all the good visionary underpinnings and we were stuck sorting through the remnants bin. Our take on rebellious youth culture amounted to Seattle Grunge culture and Euro-techno ravers. We may not have been as idealistic as the hippies who came before us, but it could have been worse. After all, we could have been pseudo-intellectual fake glasses-sporting ironic t-shirt clad hipsters.
>
> There were some vague alliances between rave culture and principles, but the connection was fuzzy at best. At its heart, rave culture represented the happy-go-lucky invincibility that characterized the 90s. You know you're getting older when you start drawing broad metaphors between youth culture and the state of the economy, but it's an aging leap I'm willing to make. Raving was youth culture in its purest, least dilute form: wild, irresponsible, and generally under contempt of adults everywhere. (Children of the 90s 2010)

Sociologically, this connection to the past makes sense. Hebdige (1979) has noted that music subcultures are always influenced by others before them, and the EDM subculture is certainly no different. However, as Matos (2015) found when conducting his interview with Neil Ollivierra, a Detroit techno musician, this took on a racialized form in the United States. As he notes:

> Mojo made it okay for young black people to listen to "white" music. . . . When they saw that was possible, they realized you could tear down similar boundaries in terms of fashion and music and literature and style and friendships and culture. They realized you could change all kinds of stuff about your life. (Matos 2015: 8)

Other early EDM musicians that we spoke with also noted that the culture at least partially emerged as a response to their marginalized status in society—at the center of which was exclusion from other cultural areas and overly oppressive policing practices popular in Detroit and Chicago. As one participant succinctly put it, "we were young, we had money, and we had no where to go where we wouldn't be harassed by law enforcement" (Female, 40, Fan).

Another significant historical event in the development of EDM took place on July 4, 1990 when Adam X, born Adam Mitchell and who was considered a founder of the New York EDM scene, painted the words P.L.U.M. (Peace, Love, Unity Movement) on a train car (Wender 2015). This term would eventually become P.L.U.R. (Peace, Love, Unity, and Respect)—a motto that became the defining feature of the EDM movement. A retelling of the story which has been widely circulated by Adam X's brother, and longtime DJ, Frankie Bones (Frank Mitchell):

> Now back to that so-called famous speech I made in The Bronx in 1993. . . . A fight breaks out between a guy and a girl and they bump right into the table all the DJ gear was on. It was on a 1960s IBM office table, so it didn't budge, but because of the memory of Happyland [a nightclub fire in the Bronx], I completely snapped. I jumped up on the table and got on the mic and addressed the situation. We never had something like this happen in 3 years. I knew everyone would understand me when I said "I'll break your f*cking faces." It was to imply I was serious. Everyone at that party knew me, so it wasn't as if I was threatening anyone with violence. The party went on into the early morning hours without incident. . . . The movement part of PLUM turned into PLUR that night by Hyperreal [an online rave chat room] 'cause the Movement was established, making the "M" become an "R" for respect. Otherwise it's one and the same. It's the only thing that connects EDM and the original scene for its duration. (Bones 2012)

One respondent that I interviewed noted that PLUR had always been embodied in the setting. In his own words:

> PLUR was always within the scene, even before it was the scene. It didn't really matter what party you went to . . . and in a way we all felt like we had to go to everyone's party because part of PLUR was supporting each other. It was expressed in a variety of ways, but it was not until the late 90s that people started using it. And even if you didn't use the term, you still followed it. (Male, 45, Fan)

PLUR also bears many similarities to the hippie counterculture, and elements of it can be found within the Clark's (1992) manifesto.

The emerging EDM culture described by Clark, and EDM enthusiasts we interviewed, encouraged experimentation in every way that might further enhance the subculture. This also extended to the production of EDM events, which challenged notions of genre and form through the use of elaborate visuals (lasers, lights, new projection technology, psychedelic imagery, etc.), a pastiche style of dress by participants, the use of non-traditional spaces for events, and the informal dissemination of event locations.[7] While critics of EDM have commented that the movement was apolitical, the counterculture was in fact very committed to advancing political ideologies, they also became politicized because of the way in which society reacted toward them. EDM events in the 1990s in L.A. for example, often faced harassment by police and other public officials. So while they were not actively organizing in the way we typically think of social movements, by holding unlicensed events where they could promote a culture focused on egalitarian ideals, these events took on a countercultural role. In the shadow of the events leading to the riots following the death of Rodney King, and due to the subculture's makeup of predominately gay Black and Latinx men in Chicago, EDM was making a powerful statement about policing 20 years before BLM protests (Silcott 1999; Reynolds 1999; McCall 2001; Collin 2009). Moreover, music anthems containing lyrics speaking about being set free were more than just hollow words. They were a response by those who felt real suffering due to their marginalized status, making EDM events a temporary escape (see Irwin 1977; Buckland 2002).

MEDIA COVERAGE

In the early 1990s, investigative journalists started to draw attention to the EDM subculture. Initially, portrayals of the subculture in America were presented primarily in television news shows and daytime talk shows. One of the earliest portrayals was on the *Today Show*. The morning news program aired a segment in 1993 titled "Raving is Latest Dance Craze" (Rappaport 1992). Instead of focusing on the deviant aspects of the culture, this clip focused on how participants of the culture dressed and danced, and their allegedly bizarre musical style. The show described the subcultural gatherings as a throwback to 1960s "love ins." The news piece only mentions drug use briefly at the end, and followed up with comments from attendees who disavowed any connection between the subculture and drug use—something that other EDM enthusiasts were also quick to note. In fact, as early reports on the subculture, like *The Today Show*, news segment, emphasized that the participants consumed far more "smart drinks" (non-alcoholic, caffeinated beverages), smoothies, water, and candies than illicit drugs. One person interviewed in *The Today Show* segment they interviewed in the report responded to inquiries about ecstasy use at raves by saying:

> People aren't just doing ecstasy at raves, they're doing them at clubs. I have nothing to do with that stuff. I think what raving is about is having a good time, meeting people, and enjoying music. (Rappaport 1992)

While *The Today Show* portrayed the EDM subculture in a positive light overall, other media portrayals were far less positive. Lifetime Network's *Jane Pratt Show* (1993) was more emblematic of most major news media coverage in its attempts to sensationalize and link ecstasy use with participation in the EDM subculture. One DJ who appeared on the show, named DB, expressed his dissatisfaction with the journalist's attempts to link ecstasy use with rave culture:

> I've been drug free for about 6 years, and I started DJing after I gave up taking drugs. For me the music is the high. . . . Um, I feel a little disappointed with this whole show, to be honest. I feel like I've sort of been brought down here under false pretenses. I thought we were here to talk about rave culture and the whole thing has been about ecstasy. (Pratt 1993)

Other so-called investigative news stories similarly emphasized the deviant aspects of the EDM movement. These programs also frequently portrayed law enforcement as inept and unable to contain their events. Moreover, they often portrayed the promoters as engaging in morally questionable, though legal, highly profitable business ventures. This sort of coverage of the subculture reflected dominant societal values as to what constituted legitimate leisure activity. However, in the shadows of the decadent 1980s, this seemed like a double standard. Despite participants' claims that drug use was not a central aspect of the EDM subculture, officials adopted the views presented in news reports that sensationalized their behavior.

INTERACTION WITH OFFICIALS

Some of the ways officials tried to control EDM events was through dance music permits, liquor licenses, and other blue laws which regulated "legitimate" spaces as well as through other bureaucratic measures such as special event permits for non-traditional spaces. Many EDM organizers who tried to go through legitimate channels were often denied. This was due largely to the fact that EDM events lasted from dusk until dawn. In response, members of the early EDM movement sought ways to circumvent the law. Some promoters would rent warehouse spaces and either lie or not fully disclose the nature of what they were doing. One promoter we interviewed talked about using the tactic of telling landlords that he owned a professional sound company (in order to explain why there might be loud music playing at night). Other promoters that we talked with said they broke into abandoned spaces—and often fled at the first sign of law enforcement.

Law enforcement and other government officials responded quickly to the sensationalized media reports, and the moral outcry of parents who perceived a link between EDM parties and drug use, by focusing on targeting the organizers of EDM events. Law-enforcement agencies utilized a variety of tactics to restrict early EDM events including juvenile curfews, fire code violations, health and safety ordinances, and liquor laws (National Drug Intelligence Center 2001). Simply put, officials treated the early EDM subculture as a threat to public safety and ultimately as a threat to the power of those in authority. This raises the question that if the media had not presented such an incompetent picture of law enforcement, would members of the subculture have faced such harassment? One early event organizer recalled that many of his events were shut down for violations of the fire code, not having the appropriate permits, and a host of other issues. As the following exchange illustrates:

Respondent: The fire department came and inspected the building. This inside building is illegal. They were going to shut us down. Plus, the fire marshal had to tell the owner of the building, "If you're making money here, you've got to take the visqueen down and all the heaters." It was freezing out. The party went on. I got a liquor permit, which allowed us to circumvent the dance laws in the city. I don't remember what time, but you had to shut down at 12, 1 am. If you have a liquor permit, you're exempt from the dance rules. So the whole goal was to circumvent the dance rules. The fire inspection, the police and all this stuff. Around 1995, I decided to buy up this space, which I believe is still empty, in order to have a dedicated venue and not have to worry about getting shut down. So I played cat and mouse with the building inspector. I always returned his calls, but I still played cat and mouse . . . in that little gray area. I got the building approved, but I made a mistake. There used to be a place where the kids had parties . . . an underground place. They got shut down, but I let them use my venue. With that came a lot of more attention from the neighborhood. I ended up with this city politician who made my life difficult. The first night, the building got raided. They came in and held all the minors, and arrested them for curfew . . . we just started the party and in 15 minutes, or maybe half hour after we started the party, they raided. Representatives from every agency you could think of, on our first night of being legal. I was arrested for maintaining a public nuisance and maintaining a business where I had knowledge of drug use.

Interviewer: Were you able to fight it and continue on?

Respondent: I hired a public defender. The public defender had a child and was very grateful that I gave space to the consortium of punk kids. This child told him how cool it was, so he asked me, "Do you want to fight this?" I said, "yeah." So the city found out I was the former secretary of state. She said I invoked the secretary of state's name. She decided to call my former boss and said what I did. My boss now happened to be the Attorney General. I'm sorry, she called the Secretary of State. It was all fishy, then this woman uses abuse of power. Not the city, chief of state and attorney general. My attorney thought that to fight this would be for abuse of power. The number of people that were arrested for controlled substance was a small fraction. Everyone was searched, like airport searched. They found a small number of people with narcotics. They held the minors until after curfew, then arrested them for curfew violation. My attorney said, "why we don't subpoena them." The chief of staff, attorney general, former U.S. Senate candidate. This was abuse of power . . . the county jail has more drugs, any basketball game has more drugs. My charges were dropped. After some bullshit. . . .but the charges were just dropped.

Interviewer: Then did you just pick up like business as usual?

Respondent: No, I did not. It broke my heart to lose that. A lot of time, a lot of money, and broke my spirit some too. We weren't doing anything that we believed was wrong. Maybe a lot of people wouldn't agree with it, but it was not immoral. (Male, 50, Promoter)

This exchange encapsulates not only the passionate drive and enthusiasm EDM promoters put into organizing their events but also the heavy-handed tactics that law-enforcement agencies would utilize to put a stop to what they perceived as a public menace. While during these formative years law-enforcement agencies would act in ways to informally put a stop to EDM gatherings, by 1995 a renewed interest in the war on drugs painted EDM gatherings as a top priority for law enforcement. One DJ offered this insight as to what changed:

It [EDM] challenged the establishment, it challenged the rock concert community, it was kids doing different things then they had done in the past. Much the same as people were afraid of rock 'n' roll when that came in the 50s and 60s. People were afraid of you know. People in the 60s were afraid of people smoking pot. In the 2000s or the 1990s people were afraid of people taking ecstasy. But it's very much the same thing as ignorance. It is hard if you're a parent with a kid who dies or gets really sick. Then of course you're going to be afraid and not want your kids to go back to these events. That is completely understandable. But consider in Europe, they went a little bit different route where they set up places for kids to test their drugs and to educate people. Here they set up laws, and tried to prevent people from going at all which then further drove it underground and then in the underground everything is completely uncontrolled. (Male, 60, DJ)

Like many EDM producers we interviewed, the above interviewee noted that because EDM was growing in popularity, it began to present a challenge to the establishment. More specifically, EDM challenged the prevailing rock concert industry, which at the time was experiencing all-time lows in attendance—yet another challenge to those in power. These powerful corporations which invest large sums of money into lobbying were threatened by EDM, which they felt were siphoning off potential profits[8]. He also notes the similarities between perceptions of rock music and marijuana usage, and the association between EDM and the drug ecstasy.

INDUSTRY PROFESSIONAL REACTIONS

One of the important ways in which early EDM events remained free from potentially co-opting outside forces was in how they were organized. While they initially were put together by groups of individuals, there was often one person in charge of bringing everything together—often referred to as the promoter. Because of their subcultural capital (see Thornton 1995), these individuals acted as important gatekeepers to their area's subculture. This type of organization made the early EDM subculture in America like fiefdoms within a larger kingdom. [9] As one respondent described it, "It was like the mafia. They were the king; it's their market. That's how they operated" (Male, 45, Promoter). The leaders of the subculture, in Weberian terms, were charismatic individuals whose power stemmed from their personality and likeability among members of the group within a given territory. Many of these early EDM promoters, such as Disco Donnie, had a funky style, but also a larger-than-life personality. Moreover, many of these individuals were revered for enchanting an otherwise dull world with fun and amusement. As one notable DJ told me:

Those parties were some of the wildest events of my life. He [the promoter] was a true visionary that cared that everyone who went to his events had a good time, but also brought something different and unique to the table. (Male, 46, DJ)

Initially at least, these early promoters were less business oriented. The chief focus was on maintaining a sense of community and adhering to the anti-consumerist sentiments of the subculture. In keeping with those principles, EDM events were produced for free or charged attendees a very modest fee (under $20).

While early members of the EDM subculture worked together to create an underground economy, nearly all the respondents I talked with noted that economic concerns were secondary. Some promoters who were perceived to be profiting from EDM events even faced repercussions from members of the scene. One EDM promoter showed the following picture (figure 1.1) and explained:

> It was a big negative for anyone to be successful in the 90s rave scene. They were mad I was charging $25. (Male, 45, Promoter)

One of the ways EDM events were kept largely free or moderately-priced produced lay in the fact that these events did not focus on looking as though they had been professionally organized. As one respondent noted:

> We didn't care how good-looking stuff was. The point was just to do it. Of course, they didn't look professional; we were lucky if they didn't shut the thing down. The point was we were there for a purpose, and that purpose wasn't a giant stage with a Moloch-looking owl. (Male, 40, Fan)

To have professionalized them would have defeated the purpose of these initial events and undermined their core values. Thus, the volunteers who came together to produce EDM events were crucial for maintaining the costs

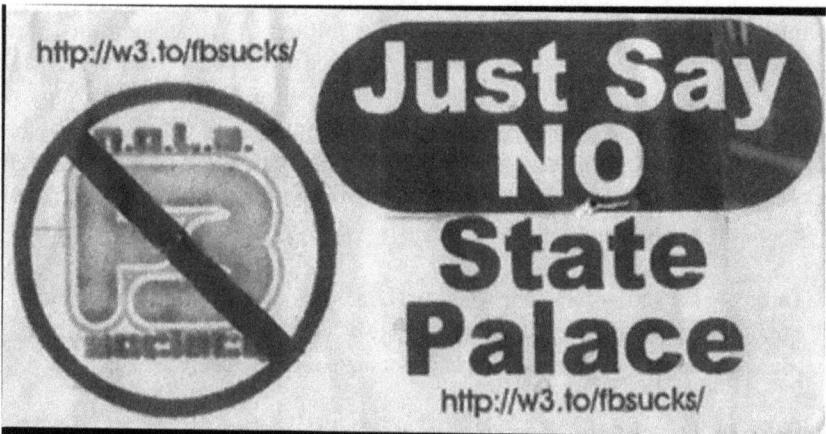

Figure 1.1 Flyer Protesting a New Orleans Rave Promotions Company. *Source*: (Twitter: @RealDiscoDonnie).

associated with producing them, and thus retaining the free-spirited communal atmosphere. Because the participants were involved in the production of their culture, they acted to protect one another as if part of a family. In the end, the result was a locally produced grassroots counterculture in which members felt intimately connected to one another.

Just as EDM spread to parts of Europe incorporating different styles, genres, distinctions, and other features, so too did it spread in the United States, acquiring different features wherever it went. For example, some organizers in New Orleans became known for creating a playful atmosphere by juxtaposing different artistic elements, creating a hodge-podge of music and art defying notions of boundaries (e.g., having a gospel choir sing hymns at the end of EDM events, puppet shows, and other interactive performers). Promoters in Minnesota and Milwaukee, for instance, added heavy metal musical and cultural influences (such as having satanic altars and other satanic iconography). Ideas that became popular were subsequently imitated and then spread, ultimately serving to unify different aspects of the subculture as common themes became repeated. There were

Figure 1.2 Flyer Depicting an *Alice in Wonderland* Themed Event, Chicago, IL. *Source:* (RavePreservationProject.Com).

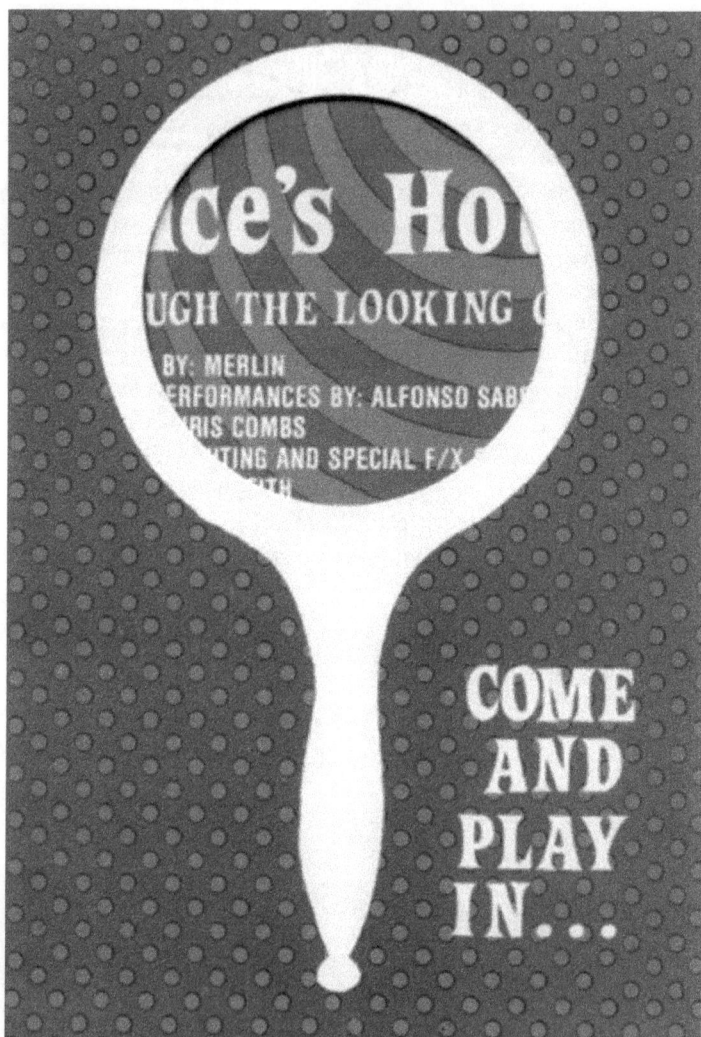

Figure 1.3 *Through the Looking Glass* **Themed Event, Los Angeles, CA.** *Source*: (RavePreservationProject.Com).

also overlaps in EDM-themed events as shown in these undated early to mid-1990s rave flyers (see figures 1.2 and 1.3). Many promoters, DJs, and others we talked to informally said that during this time period, it was not necessarily looked down upon but rather was seen as a sign of reverence, or a nod of recognition, to copy innovative ideas and concepts. One promoter explained this to us in the following way:

Yeah, we would travel to Louisville, Chicago, Dayton, Cincinnati, and sometimes beyond. You'd see something at an event and go, "Hey that's cool, I
should do that." (Female, 55, Promoter)

Some researchers have taken the localized distinctions as evidence of what
Bennett (1999) describes as a neo-tribe. Drawing upon the theoretical framework
of Maffesoli (1996), he argues that neo-tribes are a better characterization of what
sociologists have described as subcultures. Bennett's notion of neo-tribe argues
that the idea of youth culture is no longer tied to class origins, and thus we can
no longer derive meaning from the signs and symbols of these groups. Notions of
style are rendered free-floating concepts devoid of "real" meanings. Thus, neo-
tribes are composed of less definitive distinctions between insiders and outsiders,
focusing instead on loose-knit ties with fellow group members, and a lack of
commitment to a cohesive set of values. While the theory is partially accurate, it
has been used to justify the argument that no broader cohesion exists in the EDM
subculture, which our research rejects. While it may not have been uniformly

Figure 1.4   Flyer Illustrating a Party Info Line and Incorporating Childhood Characters.
Source: (RavePreservationProject.Com).

organized, the whole ethos of the subculture was built on universal acceptance. Moreover, emerging communications technologies (i.e., the Internet, email, cell phones) were allowing individuals to connect in new and important ways. Some members of the subculture reflected on this tribal connection saying:

> The word "tribe" was once used everywhere to describe rave PLUR-ality and dance collectives (Tribal Gathering, Spiral Tribe, Moontribe, Dubtribe) until ravers got sort of tribal in a bad way. No matter how much we believed we were one tribe, people always resolved to cliques. Still, everyone's heart was in the right place, and the idea that future primitives could help dream up the future was real. (Kelley 2014)

While the neo-tribe concept rests on the notion that groups that came after the 1960s are fundamentally different from their 1960s counterparts, and some degree of fluidity is always present, to some degree, in social movements, subcultures, and counterculture, one cannot simply ignore the similarities that exist between these groups.

Early EDM DJs also presented challenges to notions of authority in the way they performed and produced music. As remix artists utilizing previously recorded music, they challenged proprietary notions concerning the ownership of music (McLeod and DiCola 2011). Such concerns are the central focus of the film *Copyright Criminals* (Frazen and McLeod 2009), which was the inspiration for the book *Creative License: The Law and Culture of Digital Sampling* (McLeod and DiCola 2011). Some DJs claimed that no one owns the music, while others felt you should always obtain permission. Still, other EDM DJs felt that you should produce original music. Paradoxically, DJs and artists enjoyed a special reciprocal relationship. DJs became popular by finding new undiscovered music and artists became popular by having DJs perform and remix their work. These debates are still being waged, illustrating the politics of music, and are rooted in the free spirt of the early EDM subculture.

Advertisements for EDM subculture gatherings, or raves clearly reveal notions of anti-establishment tendencies and a sense of child-like playfulness. Many flyers and ads were designed by creating parodies of product ads found in the mainstream media. Flyer designers would repurpose these more familiar ads and then make slight modifications to subvert the original meaning. Figure 1.4, for example, shows how this was achieved by referencing popular children's literature such as Dr. Seuss, or in figure 1.5, by rebranding household items such as Windex (Spindex refers to the act of spinning records). Other ads reveal the EDM subculture's criticism of dominant society through the vision of a futuristic technologically created utopias, as in figure 1.6. Like dress and style, these flyers played a crucial role in not only conveying

Figure 1.5   EDM Flyer Depicting Anti-Consumerist Attitudes and Criticisms of Mass Culture. *Source*: (RavePreservationProject.Com).

event information, but also in promoting the values of the subculture, as well as in some cases, historical information about the DJs and performers (some flyers contained biographical information not easily obtainable through other sources).

While EDM flyers did communicate the necessary event information, they did not always identify the physical location for the events. Instead, some EDM event promoters used info lines. These were phone numbers in which prerecorded answering-machine messages gave attendees the location of the

Figure 1.6 Rave Flyer Depicting Notions of Futurism and Utopia. *Source*: (RavePreservationProject.Com).

event—sometimes updated just hours before the event. Another tactic was the utilization of map points, which were locations participants had to go in order to obtain a special map revealing the location of the event. Sometimes promoters listed several locations, making finding their events like a scavenger hunt. We also heard stories from older attendees having to obtain a password or item from secret drop locations (Ott and Herman 2003). This allowed EDM promoters to elude law-enforcement threats, and to keep the events exclusive to members of the subculture.

Sociologically speaking, notions of authenticity can be a loaded term. Many often fall into the trap of thinking authenticity is an either/or concept, and such logics, as we found, dominate much of EDM. However, as Hidalgo (2022) argues, authenticity is a constructed process that is ongoing and ever changing. It is also an embodied process that is often never directly discussed, but rather like the DJs, promoters, and other industry professionals we talked with, is articulated as part of one's outward performance of self. Those who were part of the organization of EDM talked about being involved with the organization of EDM events and the importance of "being in it for the right reasons," which is often a phrase used within the business and organization of EDM to refer to more altruistic motives—for the scene, because of a passion for the music, or other similar phrases were also used This topic was even discussed at the 2010 annual EDMbiz Conference, where a panel on the topic of authenticity reflected on this notion:

Moderator: There are actually people in this panel who actually embody what Simon is saying [authenticity]. Simon, when you started out as a journalist, which I'm sure was high up for low return. I'm sure you got numerous blogs before you came, before you became the editor in chief of Thumb. When you started in 1992, it was more for the passion of music, not the dollars. I still believe there are people out there doing it for the right reasons. However, I feel that it's been overshadowed by trying to make a quick buck.

Panelist A: But I think there's more to it than that. I used to be invited to parties all the time to raise money for a cause, whether that was for Hurricane Katrina or Aids awareness or something small and personal, like someone's personal health crisis. You don't really see those things anymore. I think it's hard to reconcile the ethos of EDM, and certainly it's EDM's business which has defined success of a singular thing with the idea that of us being a community that also cares about the future and legacy and the quality of life for not just ourselves, but the entire world . . .

During this panel, and in the excerpt above, you can see a reflection and a longing for a past which they viewed as being purer. Note that 2010 was the year in which the largest North American Dance Music festival, The Electric Daisy Carnival, moved to Las Vegas Nevada, and EDM became a recognized genre at the Grammy Awards Ceremony. These panelists noted that EDM events used to focus more on social good via fundraisers for larger causes, but also for more localized charitable acts. Ultimately, they were noting how early EDM events in these formative years rejected, even if only tangentially, placing profits above the values of the subculture.

Like the Goths in Hodkinson's (2002) study, authenticity was also maintained by creating an underground economy—spending money within the subculture, and only spending money outside of the culture when absolutely necessary. According to one DJ:

> We created economies of scale [an informal economy]. I remember talking to Rick Thompson, and back then they talked about how he would pay this guy some money for these lights, and then this guy paid him money for design, then he paid me money for doing some stuff, and I bought records at the record store owned by other guys in the scene. It was all interesting how the money circulated in our own economy. It went other places too, but certainly it kept circulating. You can kind of do that; you can be intentional about that. I want to rent a sound system from someone I know that's busting their ass and has been buying great sound equipment. Well, let's hire them so they can buy great sound equipment. So you know someone who knows the music who is doing sound. You want a flyer design; ask a DJ who graduated with a degree in graphic design. Don't hire outside. You can keep that money circulating if you're intentional about it. (Female, 40, DJ)

Thus, individual contributions were made out of a sense of loyalty to other members, and a feeling of commitment to something larger than oneself. Others I spoke with expressed similar sentiments such as "supporting their friends," because "they [the event organizers or performers] were cool people," due to "who might show up," or "to support the scene." So, while utilizing informal networks resulted in an underground economy, its main purpose was to support those committed to the creation of the subculture. DJs reflecting on how they got their start in their careers noted that they were often paid very little to perform, had to sleep on friends' sofas, and made agreements with little more than a handshake. This was true even for DJs who were critically acclaimed within the EDM subculture at that time.

Another way in which members of the EDM subculture maintained notions of authenticity was through highlighting individuals' artistic innovation or in innovation through other forms of creativity. Moreover, in the early formative years, becoming a DJ was a difficult task due to a lack of professional equipment requiring specialized knowledge about the subculture, which sociologists refer to as subcultural capital (Thoronton 1996). Early DJs thus became known for their creative talents, especially their ability to innovate, which often involved inventing their own machines to produce and perform music. As one DJ recalls:

At the time, we didn't have BPM counter and meat matching. Remember, this was pre-technic 1200 [one of the most popular turntables still somewhat in use today by DJs]. So what we had to do was find consumer turntables that had a pitch control. Usually, they had a + or a – which allowed you to adjust the pitch. So if you were really good, you could go + + - + - - and make two records sync up. You memorized the beats of your records to know what you needed to do. We tried all kinds of things, cutting reel to reel tapes, etc. The other thing you would do is take the metal piece on the turntable and manipulate it to adjust the pitch. This is a far cry from what you are capable of doing today. (Male, 60, DJ)

An interview with an EDM DJ reflecting on this time period described the difficulty in similar ways:

Speaking of primitive, mixing used to be fucking hard. It took full concentration just to match beats, much less take people on a seamless journey. It took hard-earned cash to buy turntables and a mixer and to build a record collection. DJs had to hunt for vinyl at specialty record stores tucked away in big cities. There was no Beatport, no SoundCloud, and no Discogs. DJing was a labor of love by default. Because it was, you could hear the revolution in the music. (Kelley 2014)

Another DJ we interviewed described DJing as a "painful process that involved splicing tape, experimenting with new equipment that might or might not pan out, and having to come up with solutions on the spot. The best way I can describe it was its like walking a tight rope without any safety equipment." (Male, 50, DJ)

The difficulty in being a DJ in the early EDM subculture thus created several barriers preventing outsiders from entering. Producers of original dance music sometimes stumbled upon equipment that they could manipulate into producing a desired effect. One example of a machine that was repurposed this way was the 303, which was initially designed for Karaoke. Early music producers found out that by using it in a way for which it was not designed, they could create new kinds of electronic sounds (Hindmarch 2001). Other producers created their own elaborate musical contraptions, such as Mr. Quintron's light machine (see figure 1.7). Quintron was known for his many inventions, including a light-activated drum machine—fulfilling an artistic need but also creating a spectacle for the audience—something which would be of significant importance as EDM developed.

While compact discs toward the end of this era began to become popular, DJs preferred to play on vinyl. In fact, it wouldn't be until much later that CD turntables would enter the market, allowing DJs to manipulate them. Even still, manufacturing new releases on vinyl sharply declined. This was a huge problem

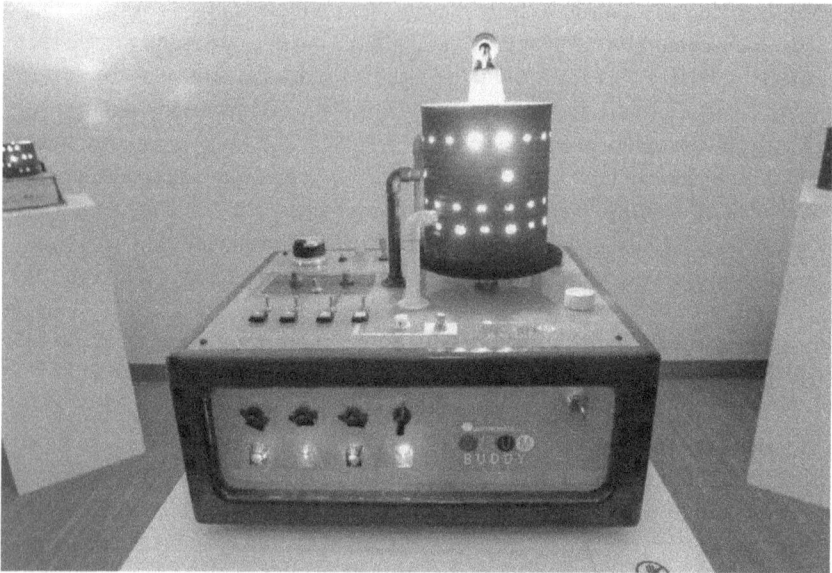

Figure 1.7   Mr. Quintron's Drum Buddy. *Source*: (Galveston Arts Center).

for the EDM scene. Previously, most record labels only produced limited runs, making a DJs collection the basis upon which they would earn subcultural capital. Ever rarer vinyl releases meant that DJs had to compete to for new releases, and they became increasingly judged on the rarity of their collections. Some DJs that we talked to also referred to the importance of owning rare, pre-release records called "white labels." White label albums, which consisted of early released or limited release compositions, could only be obtained through connections to the music producers themselves. Thus, one's music collection was a matter of both luck and how connected a DJ was to the music industry.

With the internet still in its early days, EDM DJs and performers took on a pivotal role as gatekeepers to the music. While today a variety of technological innovations have occurred making it easy to hear DJ performances, in these early days the only way to find this genre of music was to either attend a live event or to be gifted a cassette recording of DJs performance. Like the Jam Band Scene (i.e., Grateful Dead and Phish), musical recordings were used primarily among those in the subculture, were rarely monetized and were often of poor quality. This meant that if you found EDM musically appealing, you had to attend a live event. As such, live performing DJs were often more important than the artists' music they were actually playing. This was also due in part to the lack of identifiers in early EDM. As one of our respondents noted,

Yeah, back in the early days, we didn't know who anyone was or the names of any of the tracks. You couldn't buy a dance music CD in those days like you can now, or go online and find stuff. So I remember one of the first artists that took off had this track and the only word in it was dominator, and the whole song just repeated the word over and over. (Male, 45, Promoter)

Even if you were in attendance, interrupting a DJ's performance was a faux pas that even today is met with serious sanctions. The consensus among those we interviewed was that this helped preserve maintain artistic quality of the music, by rejecting notions of celebrity.

DJs themselves were often placed in dimly-lit corners or off to the side—in marked contrast to today's multimillion-dollar spectacles where they are placed at the center of attention. This meant that the focus was more on the DJ's skill and ability as a performer. Even if a DJ was placed center stage, they would usually be surrounded by decorations that obscured rather than highlighted their performance. Cameras, which were used in projected visuals, focused on their hands (the main way DJs manipulated records), rather than their faces. The only qualifiers that might differentiate early EDM performers, outside of their talent, came from their geographical location (i.e., a DJ coming from the UK to play in the US), or because they incorporated some kind of special gimmick that was advertised on the flyers—not unlike the one pictured in figure 1.7. In this early era, notions of being a superstar DJ (known only for their name recognition) were virtually non-existent.

One early event organizer we interviewed, reflecting on the intimacy of the early EDM subculture, talked about the network of individuals he relied upon in order to make his events happen. His group consisted of approximately six individuals in charge of various event aspects such as venue, lighting, sound, DJs, decorations, and flyers. In his own words:

The main difference between today's EDM scene and the early days was that these events produced a sense of family; they weren't about making money, and we were all equal . . . not only the people attending, but the people making these things happen. (Male, 35, Promoter).

Thus, these events were communal and produced from shared group resources. It is perhaps this characteristic which drew early adopters to the subculture—the yearning for a place where they could feel a sense of belonging.

FAN REACTIONS

While the producers of EDM are without a doubt one of the most important elements of the subculture, the fans also make up an important aspect of the culture. Like early EDM professionals, the fans consisted primarily of Queer Black and Latinx men living in Chicago and Detroit—though this would soon extend to other areas like New York City, New Orleans, and, eventually, Los Angeles. Within these urban incubators, the culture grew and made use of the increasing decline in manufacturing which provided empty warehouses that became inhabited by EDM enthusiasts eager to listen to music and dance the night away. These early EDM events were characterized, in the literature and by those we spoke with, as intimate affairs with attendance ranging from a few hundred to as many as several thousand people. Even at large-scale events, our respondents felt that they were far more organic and intimate—yet its hard to know if this is nostalgia or if a qualitative difference actually existed. We maintain that the importance is how these events are remembered, even if a distortion it says something interesting about the current state of the EDM subculture.

Another major defining characteristics of the early EDM subculture was the willingness of members to challenge the official rules and reject societal values prevalent at the time. Their critical political orientation and free-spirited nature, coupled with media accounts linking them with drug use (which we discuss later), meant that, in the eyes of outsiders, those associated with EDM were members of a deviant subculture. Sociologist Stanley Cohen (1972) has also referred to this process as a moral panic—a process by which the media exaggerates the deviant aspects of the group, making them into scapegoats for other societal problems, otherwise known as "folk devils." Similarly, other sociologists argue that their active resistance to the rules of society differentiates them, and other groups like them, as countercultures (Yinger 1960; Fine and Kleinman 1979; Panfil 2017).

Many have wrongfully characterized early EDM culture as being apolitical—due to its emphasis on "free love" as expressed in PLUR. However, the early EDM subculture in fact had a variety of politically subversive counter-cultural aspects embedded within it. This is perhaps best expressed by one of our interview respondents:

> I've always been an anti-establishment kind of guy. I was always involved with liberal politicians . . . you should have the right to have private property to do what you want. Why does the government have a say what time you dance to? So, definitely we were just trying to live free. We weren't necessarily trying to change the world. We were trying to create a place . . . a utopian society existing inside the larger world. (Male, 60, Promoter)

Or this blogger who recalled:

> Dancing to electronic dance music was a liberation that broke the mold. Old school ravers danced with a primal freedom that often scared those looking in . . . Rave came along in the computer age, during the dawn of the internet, and before the trauma of 9/11. It freed minds and got asses moving. (Kelley 2014)

The openness and accepting nature, embedded in the idea of PLUR, made it attractive to a variety of other marginalized groups. Thus, early EDM subculture events were made up of a diverse array of individuals who were simultaneously looking for spaces centered on allowing others to express themselves in a tolerant environment. These included individuals discriminated against because of their gender, sexual orientation, class, race, religion, or other identity markers.

Like the artists who had to devote considerable time and money into learning how to DJ, fans also had to go out of their way in order to attend EDM events. Often going to an EDM event in this era meant you had to be invited by someone, go to a specialty record store, or somehow be "in the know." Another factor detouring casual outsiders was in the hoops that fans had to jump through to find the actual location of an EDM event. The process as one blogger described, it involved:

> Pagers, answering machines, tape decks, landlines, paper fliers, zines—there was no internet at rave's genesis. You had to know someone to get the number that got you to the party that got you a flier that got you to the next party. Pagers, hotlines, and answering machines helped grease the wheels. Back then, word of mouth was actually word of mouth.
>
> Things like map points—a second or sometimes third location you had to find to get final directions to an underground party—along with three to four-hour drives to a rave were part of the adventure. No festivals hosted this music; you had to go the distance. These twists and turns were a ritual that added to the anticipation and excitement. They told you the future was in front of you. (Kelley 2014)

Many of the people we spoke with enjoyed the urban scavenger hunts. Several contemporary club owners catering to EDM enthusiasts, would produce events that were throwbacks to such urban scavenger hunts—trying to recapture the mystique of the early days. However, these hoops also helped keep EDM events out of the prying eyes of public officials and law-enforcement agencies. As one participant recalled:

> Sometimes you would go to the party and it would either be shut down, or you had to embark on a kind of urban scavenger hunt to find the party. There was more than one time we spent the entire night driving around trying to find the party because we couldn't figure out the maps or because we'd been given bogus directions. (Male, 40, Fan)

Thus, despite their best efforts, early EDM gatherings were often shut down or faced significant logistical problems such as power outages or inadequate sound equipment.

Figure 1.8   A Desert Rave Illustrating Different Styles of Dress 1998. *Source*: (Michael Tullberg).

Figure 1.9   EDM Participants at a Desert Rave. *Source*: (Michael Tullberg).

Subculture researchers have pointed to dress and style as one of the hallmarks of authenticity within music subcultures (Wiltsher 2016). Members of the early EDM subculture, however, wore a variety of different styles, which Mary Grace Cerni (2014), an *LA Weekly* reporter, discussed as a continuum. At one extreme, early EDM participants wore overalls, tie-dye shirts, plastic beads, Adidas shoes, baggy pants, and t-shirts. An example of this kind of style can be seen in figure 1.8 and figure 1.9 (Tullberg 2014). This style of dress allowed early EDM participants to dance more comfortably. At the other end of the spectrum were styles featuring exaggerated notions of play and fantasy. Members sometimes used makeup and other theatrics to make

Figure 1.10 Example of EDM Participants as Unique Characters. *Source*: (Michael Tullberg).

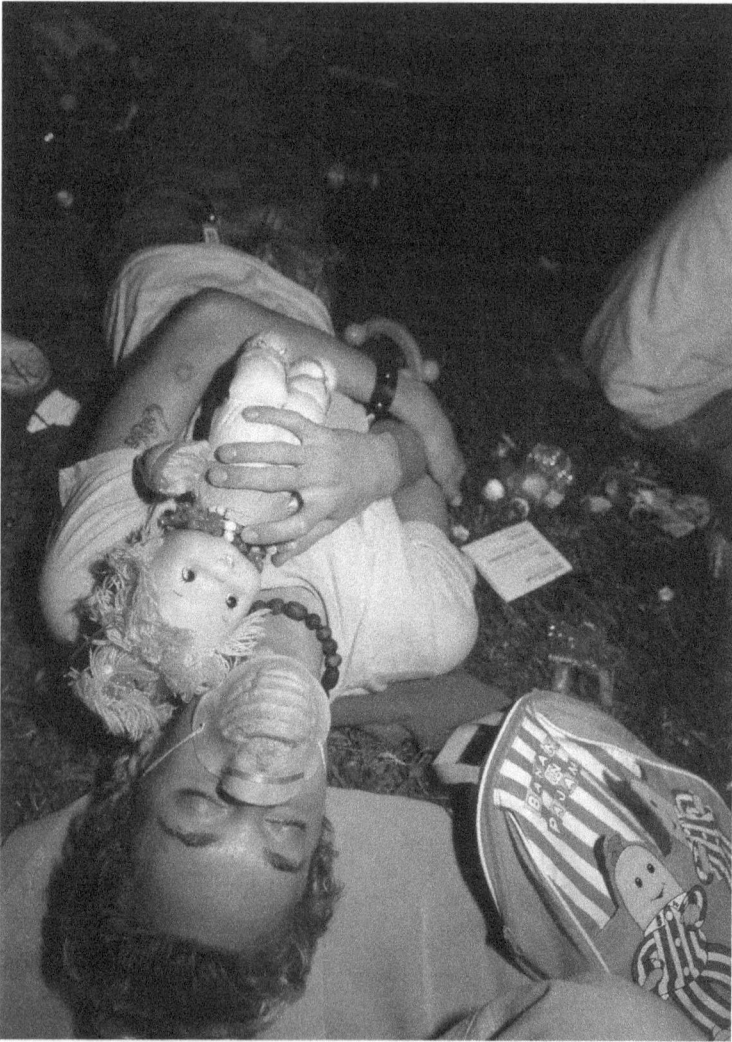

Figure 1.11   Depiction of Kandi Ravers. *Source*: (Michael Tullberg).

themselves into a kind of unique character (see figure 1.10). Others were
known as Kandi kids (see figure 1.11). Kandi kids were characterized by
their brightly colored clothing and bright beaded jewelry resembling candy
necklaces given to children.

Like most of the other facets of the subculture, dress and style were appropriated from other subcultures. This makes talking about a precise notion
of style and dress particularly challenging. Despite such an array of styles,
there are some common features which can be gleaned from looking at these

different styles. The particular messages embedded in their style included notions of playfulness, youthfulness, and, as some discussed with me, the reclamation of their childhoods. These notions, especially playfulness, are also embedded in the event flyers pictured earlier.

CONCLUSION

The early years of the EDM subculture laid the foundation for a vibrant underground music subculture. This early counterculture challenged authority, appropriated abandoned warehouses spaces, sought to challenge the established order and sparked an international social movement. The values of the movement were first articulated as PLUM but would later become better known as PLUR . While many credit the cultural elements as originating from EDM's cross-pollination with Europeans, we found that the core values, like the music, were first codified by American enthusiasts. However, there can be no doubt that European influences were necessary to help develop and popularize the subculture. The style of dress, flyers, and many other aspects of EDM culture focused around youthfulness and also playfulness. Early EDM enthusiasts could be clearly identified by their brightly colored clothing, which drew upon elements of hip-hop and other subcultures.

Demographically speaking, many of the early adherents to the culture were already marginalized members as gay men of color. As such, much of what the early EDM subculture was responding to was the oppression that comes from being marginalized and alienated from the dominant culture. As a Midwest urban phenomenon, the role of policing, redlining, and other forms of structural discrimination cannot be overstated (Rothstein 2017). As such, the early EDM subculture's focus on PLUR was more than lip service. Some EDM producers, promoters, and cultural icons made powerful statements on the role of marginalized persons—even if others downplayed these aspects. Thus, as a counterculture they were resisting conformity to a system which they felt perpetuated inequalities based on race, class, gender, and sexual orientation.

Exaggerated media reports and subsequent responses by legal and political authorities treated the EDM subculture as a threat to society or, in sociological terms, a moral panic. This response by public officials had a disproportionate impact upon queer men of color. Often portrayed as little more than a deviant drug-using subculture, the EDM subculture was made into a folk devil—a scapegoat for what was perceived as a prevalent drug problem in society (Cohen 1972). While this strategy was successful in demonizing hip-hop and other popular music genres at the time, such stigmas would be largely overcome by EDM, as we will show in preceding chapters. Nonetheless, in these early formative years, those involved with EDM found ways to subvert official efforts to prevent them from gathering.

Despite these official viewpoints, the EDM subculture was in fact focused on a commitment to the notions of PLUR and a future society, aided by technological innovation aimed at eliminating social inequalities. Its members resisted efforts to contain them and invested a great deal of time in order to maintain control of the culture they were creating. Fans, DJs, and promoters all earned respect according to how closely they followed these core values. The initial gatherings of the EDM subculture were produced with an emphasis on artistic and creative aspects over conventional notions of professionalism.

A number of factors played an important role in facilitating the development of a second phase in the EDM subculture. The first factor facilitating this evolution came from the popularization of the subculture, largely due to increased media attention. While the media did not intend to do so, it inadvertently exposed a wider audience to this emerging subculture. The result was that EDM events, which originally attracted, at most, a few hundred people would mushroom to several thousand attendees. Second, and most importantly, this increased growth led to increased friction with the media, politicians, and other officials. This culminated in the mobilization of law-enforcement entities to charge EDM promoters under laws intended to close down crack houses. As we will unpack in the next chapter, attempts at passing new legislation aimed specifically at EDM events and spearheaded by then Senator Joseph R. Biden, would make EDM public enemy number one.

NOTES

1. Including the continental baths, a chain of gay bathhouses (see Maestro 2003; Higgins 2013).

2. As Brewster and Broughton (2000) have pointed out, hip-hop was also a major inspiration for this genre. Hip-hop artists developed the technique of using turntables as a way of creating music. So much of the technique was inspired by musicians within that genre. This may help explain why, initially, early EDM artists were African American men, oftentimes working out of gay clubs (see also Thomas 1995; Silcott 1999).

3. Interestingly, garage music, an offshoot of house music, was also so named because of its home at the Paradise Garage in New York (a gay club at 84 King Street). Most EDM historians either emphasize one or the other.

4. While the term "Queer" has become highly popularized, especially within studies of sexuality, at the time this term wasn't necessarily popular among members of the subculture or the larger LGBT movement.

5. As observed in shirts bearing cartoon logos, stuffed animals, and pacifiers.

6. Though many authors point out the drug connection, they also point out that not everyone took drugs, arguing that the events themselves were enough of a stimulus for many participants.

7. Early rave events would utilize party info lines sometimes announcing the location only hours before the actual event or map point locations whereby one had to go to a series of locations to find out the event locale.

8. An EDM promoter we interviewed noted that a Clear Channel representative in his market felt threatened by the popularization of the subculture.

9. This is a point which is important in the third phase. While in this first phase there are a variety of promoters, they eventually come to be dominated by only a handful of people—bought up and merged into corporately owned EDM promotion groups.

Chapter 2

Phase II: The Rise of the Rave Outlaw (1995–2009)

From 1995 to 2009, the structural makeup of the electronic dance music (EDM) subculture transitioned away from its original countercultural beginnings. During this phase of the subculture, EDM promoters began utilizing nightclubs and other "legitimate" music venues. This shift emerged primarily as the result of ongoing police harassment, which was brought on due to increased negative publicity from the media. The 1990s was fraught with increased news coverage and competition for viewership (Victor 1993). Talk shows like Geraldo Rivera, Sally Jesse Raphael, Jenny Jones, and Ricky Lake made their mark by offering their viewers sensationalized accounts of human behavior. Toward the middle of the decade EDM promoters, enthusiasts, and DJs became regular guests, and late-night local television outlets ran "investigative" pieces which focused almost exclusively on the "deviant" if not illicit aspects of the subculture (Owen 2003). While such media coverage also happened in the previous era, it was mixed in its depiction of EDM. Now, media coverage uniformly portrayed EDM as a menace to society.

By reporting on the EDM subculture in increasingly sensationalized ways, the media acted as an amplifier, drawing increased participation by those unaware that these events were even happening. Moreover, such media accounts were tapping into underlying racial and queer panics that were ongoing throughout this time period—and arguably still exist today (Conner and Katz 2020; Conner and Okamura 2021a, 2021b; Conner and MacMurray 2022; Conner and Dickens 2022). The rise in popularity meant parents were also placing increased pressure on public officials (politicians and law-enforcement agents) to respond. Thus, the shift into public venues such as nightclubs, fairgrounds, and other licensed venues was both an attempt to quell public outcry and also a response to the increasingly large crowds lured in by those watching these journalistic accounts.

Even before public outcry emerged, the sudden increase in attendance at EDM events began to produce significant challenges for promoters. In short, using clandestine, often illegally obtained spaces (i.e., warehouses, cornfields, desert spaces) became unfeasible. The infrastructure "underground" spaces, which were often not intended for the purposes they were used for, often lacked bathroom facilities, access to water, or adequate space for the thousands of people attending them. Organizers that we spoke with talked of growing concerns as to the safety of participants at their events and they realized quickly that greater infrastructure was needed to handle these massive gatherings. As one promoter explained:

> Everybody realized that we had to get legitimate, because basically we had 600 people with no security, no liquor license. At some point, any human being is going to be like, "oh shit, this is dangerous. I'm going to get fucking sued, right?" There is a tipping point. (Male, 40, Promoter)

While many critics argue that this dramatically altered the culture and purpose of EDM events, some noted that this tradeoff did have its benefits. As one EDM professional pointed out:

> I went to a party in New York City. It was either '95 or '96. An Electric Zoo type of event. We drove from New Orleans to go to this party. It was huge, with 70,000 people. To us, the best thing ever, right? It was at a stadium and legitimized. Not a dingy warehouse. Could get shut down. In the 90s, when it really got legit, is when I moved to these bigger venues. It became an overall better experience for people involved. It's not like a warehouse, Porta-potties, no safety, no insurance, no liquor license. It'd grown too big and we moved into legitimate venues to help make it grow. (Male, 40, Promoter)

Another promoter we spoke with echoed these sentiments, but notes the difficulty in trying to explain this to his audiences:

> When we first started using the State Palace Theater in New Orleans, it was a lot of blowback. Now we're on Ticketmaster, magazine ads, radio ads, and people were like, this is bullshit, you sold out, but the venue was amazing and was a lot safer. Easier to deal with, we didn't have power shutdowns, security, not being underground anymore. There were some constraints on the tickets, stuff like that. There was just a whole lot of negative flow from the fans sometimes. (Male, 40, Promoter)

However, this shift also meant that promoters had to start charging fees and abiding by the rules of the venues they were occupying. This would prove to be a tough sell to a group which had become accustomed to gatherings that had either a very modest admission fee or were free. Thus, the participants in the culture were caught in a contradiction between their anti-capitalist values and their ideological devotion toward participating in cultural gatherings.

ONGOING DEVELOPMENTS

While the police had started to become involved in the EDM subculture in its formative years, with the shift into licensed venues provided some protection. It was after all much easier to break up an unlicensed gathering than to shut down an event held in a licensed music venue. While some law-enforcement agencies continued to monitor the activities of EDM enthusiasts, for the most part they were left to their own devices. However, the move into legitimate licensed venues was in part an evasion tactic by promoters trying to resist law-enforcement initiatives, it also subverted some of the cultural mechanisms that allowed it to remain true to its core values. Licensed venues like bars and nightclubs are first and foremost privately owned spaces concerned with consumption. They are what some scholars call third spaces—open to the public but privately owned (Lofland 1998). As such, EDM promoters were only able to utilize those spaces if they could prove themselves to be profitable to the owners. Thus, by bringing EDM into these more public spaces they initiated a transition away from organizing around subcultural capital (Thornton 1996). The promoters themselves began to grow concerned with how they were funding their events, their profitability, and other business-oriented aspects.

Another major development in the development of EDM was the increased presence of outsiders, particularly those involved in the corporate music industry. As they were now utilizing some of the same event spaces used by rock and pop musicians, advertising to mass audiences, and branding themselves, music industry professionals became aware of this developing music subculture. As promoters increasingly began to sell out these same venues, these executives saw potential profits. One music executive we interviewed had the following to say:

R: the thing to keep in mind is we were all losing our minds quietly behind the scenes. Revenues were down, people were getting laid off, and everyone was worried they would lose their jobs. A friend of mine who worked for Sony, [name redacted for anonymity], was told on Friday he was being let go, and by 5 pm that afternoon his email was turned off and his work cell was disconnected. All of the contacts he had built up over the last decade or so just gone. Poof.

I: And this was all because of EDM?

R: In part . . . I mean it's hard to know for certain but, things were shifting. You had Napster, a decline in CD sales, and we were looing for the next big musical innovation that we could absorb and profit off. But, it was hard... and we just couldn't do it. We didn't understand what we were doing. The promoters controlled the scene and we were trying to plug what they were doing into our formula, but that wasn't EDM. That whole scene was organic, and the model we were trying to use grew out of rock... it just wasn't the same. It was also like super localized, and our formula was built on mass production. (Female, 47, Music Industry Executive)

In other words, EDM became a source of interest for agents of the music industry. As the executive notes, larger shifts in technology and music production were destabilizing the traditional, if not transactional, structure of the music industry, a topic we will return to later in this chapter. However, because EDM was founded on anti-consumerist and anti-capitalist ideas, it proved challenging to co-opt. While promoters were being featured on major network television news shows, major record labels struggled to capitalize on what looked like to them, the largest cultural phenomenon since the 1960s hippie culture. Much of their "failure" was due to the fact that music labels were trying to capitalize on EDM through album sales. EDM DJs were known not for songs, but for their live, often eight hour performances. This would change in 1993, when record companies began to produce EDM events.

In the early days of the EDM subculture, the internet was in its infancy, but in this phase it became a much more widely utilized tool to connect with others. As one participant we interviewed recalled:

In the Bay area in the 90s there was a huge crossover between the tech industry and rave culture. You also had a lot of tech bros who had money to burn so they would either spend it throwing massive parties or by spending it a clubs for bottle service for their friends and co-workers. So if you were a DJ in those days you were thriving and making bank. (Male, 45, DJ)

Thus, it would appear that EDM's development in this era owed a lot to direct financial contributions from those involved in the dot com boom. However, other respondents we talked with emphasized the importance of the internet for dissemination of music in the genre and for finding the location of EDM events. In one participant's words:

The internet played a huge role in making rave popular. All the sudden you had kids headed to college and looking for something to do and the promoters made lists on sites like yahoo groups. This really helped make it spread. You also had a lot of people trading music. Now you didn't have to go to a record store to find out about parties, you could just sign up for an email list. You also had sites like

Bluelight spring up that discussed all types of things that were going on in the scenes like how to properly use drugs, where you could find raves in your area, and other ways of connecting with other rave kids. (Female, 50, DJ/Promoter)

As the above participant notes, the internet allowed for the dissemination of the culture in new and unexpected ways. This is also something discussed by Tammy Anderson (2009a), who notes that while this gave greater connectivity, it also made it more accessible to outsiders. Among the outsiders who began to take notice were those working within major record labels and who were searching for new artists.

The earliest EDM touring show hosted by a major record label was the "Rave New World Tour" in 1993. Produced by Elektra Records (a subsidiary of Time Warner), this major record label wanted to test the waters to see if they could break into the EDM market. The Rave New World Tour featured a variety of acts, most of whom began as underground DJs performing for incredibly low fees by today's standards. The tour consisted of thirteen North American cities, including Washington DC, New York, Philadelphia, Boston, Montreal, Toronto, Detroit, Chicago, Indianapolis, Denver, El Paso, Los Angeles, and San Francisco. While those we interviewed reported that the tour underperformed in terms of music executives' expectations, and upset longtime EDM enthusiasts, it had a huge secondary impact by helping popularize the EDM genre, with massive amounts of advertising dollars spent in major media markets across the United States. Moreover, additional dates were added, expanding the tour to 26 total tour dates.

Another important development that came from the underperformance of the first leg of the tour was that executives began to experiment to find the right formula for American audiences. Their solution was to add in groups that might be appealing to both rock audiences, who were unfamiliar with EDM, and participants of the subculture. Two rock-oriented groups The Prodigy and Moby were added and proved to be highly successful in making EDM more accessible to mainstream audiences. The sound of these groups not only mimicked aspects of EDM but also incorporated elements of live musicians that were more familiar to American audiences. After the success of the second leg of the tour, a follow-up one called "See the Light" was scheduled the same year in order to provide record executives with confirmation that they had formulated a way to produce EDM gatherings.

Beyond marking the entry of major recording labels to EDM, the significance of the "Rave New World" and "See the Light" tours was that they led to a significant shift in the public perception of EDM. The genre had previously been marginalized due to its roots in the gay club scene, but the introduction of electronic groups that mimicked live music meant that it could be repackaged and produced in a way that was more marketable. Those who we talked to who went to the "Brave New World" tour noted the confusion audiences experienced. According to those we talked with, the sites were often traditional concert venues with rows of seats, making dancing nearly impossible. Moby, for instance, utilized live keyboards and The Prodigy consisted of a traditional rock band (i.e., a guitarist, singer, drummer). However, unlike traditional rock acts, they both utilized electronic synthesized beats and DJ equipment (laptops, keyboard, DJ equipment). In short, the whole production apparatus of the music industry began to shift to accommodate EDM.

At the same time, a new form of EDM had developed that incorporated hip-hop elements. Known as "breaks" or "break beats," this genre began to turn hip-hop audiences onto EDM. Groups like DJ Icey and The Dust Brothers (later known as The Chemical Brothers) were combining rock, hip-hop, and EDM, while also experimenting with audiovisual lighting and projection techniques. Errol Kolosine, an EDM industry label professional, explained the importance of this:

> The Brothers' live show offered salvation. Black people, white people, gay people, straight people, frat boys—you name it. Everybody here is equal, and the music is what is bringing everybody in here together. It occurred to me, if I get enough people to experience this, we can't lose. (cited in Matos 2015: 213)

To some this appeared as encroachment by music executives, to others it looked like an organic development in the culture. Regardless, the end result was that the mainstream music industry and EDM were becoming more tightly interwoven and also as a result, the presence of EDM more widely known.

The involvement of major music corporations also opened up a variety of other avenues to EDM artists. For the first time ever, due in part to the afore-mentioned tours, EDM artists were being played on radio stations (Matos 2011, 2015). Also, some EDM groups began to receive significant recognition in 1997, and major film studios started to take note, licensing EDM artists for their music. The Crystal Method was one of the first groups to achieve such recognition. Following the 1997 release of their album, *Vegas*, an homage to their native city, the group began receiving licensing deals from major film studios, as did other artists outside the EDM genre seeking to update their sound. EDM was thus crossing over. Many promoters recalled this time period with great enthusiasm. In their minds, they were receiving recognition for the hard work they had put in, but, more importantly, they still also had some autonomy from the major corporate entities. Indeed, the first EDM tours were only possible due to partnerships with local promoters.

DJs, fans, promoters, and others involved in the subculture we spoke with pointed to the rise of trance music as a sign of just how much the mainstream music model had come to influence the EDM subculture. The top grossing DJs toward the end of this era were predominantly trance and progressive house (a fusion of house and trance) music DJs. Trance music was one of the first post 1990s EDM genres to include vocals in the production of songs. While early house music used vocals, it was rare for vocals to be used in the late 1990s. Trance musical compositions changed that. Trance music is best characterized by its harmonic melodies, its use of predominantly white female vocalists, and a more standardized format than most other genres of EDM. The genre in many ways resembled a fusion of classical music theory, pop music, and elements unique to EDM (use of synthesizers and other computer-created sounds).

The sociological significance of the development of trance music was that it signaled yet another way that EDM was becoming a mainstream phenomenon. What some saw as the hyper fracturing of EDM into multiple genres, was actually just continued experimentation, often by those within the corporate music industry, to draw in as many people as possible. Trance DJs, unlike house and techno musicians, played around the world and toured the United States in lavish tour buses. Trance events were held in massive venues, ranging in capacity from 1,000 to 10,000 persons. Some popular DJs would sell out venues in minutes, and often played multiple dates in areas like Chicago, where this style of music was particularly popular due to the large Eastern European immigrant population. Other DJs, noticing this shift, began producing lyrically infused songs and became known as trance musicians. Trance became known as the pop music of EDM, and techno and house DJs began to feel eclipsed and marginalized.

This shift in style also contained a racialized aspect. House and techno DJs were predominantly persons of color and those who performed trance sets were predominantly white Europeans from the Netherlands, Sweden, Germany, Russia, and Poland. These new DJs were also highly conscious about their image, prominently displaying pictures of themselves (on album covers or in the liner notes), and by hiring professional photographers to enhance their image. This flew in the face of the principles of the original EDM subculture in which beauty, sex appeal, and glamorization of one's image were frowned upon. Thus, notions of authenticity, branding, and the other issues discussed in this chapter concerns the emerging encroachment of a largely white outside audience appropriating Black and Latinx urban culture.

MEDIA COVERAGE

The media and EDM have always had a tense relationship, ranging from dismissing it as a youth fad that would soon fizzle out, to frightful depictions of it that preyed upon parent's fears. In this second era, however, the media played an even far more prominent role in shaping public perception toward the genre, intensely covering EDM gatherings. Respected mainstream outlets such as *USA Today* began reporting on the "growing nuisance" of EDM events, and TV sitcoms such as *90210* referenced EDM and ecstasy use (Matos 2015). Daytime talk shows would also invite EDM promoters and enthusiasts on their programs. Some individuals that we interviewed suggested that promoters were likely "working the media," leaning into stereotypes in order to be seen on the national stage. Others we spoke with felt as though talk show hosts were sensationalizing and taking advantage of the naivety of willing participants. Regardless of intent, the effect was the same—EDM became associated with something to be feared in the minds of parents and public officials.

As EDM began to grow in this era, aspiring EDM DJs began to seek alternative ways they could participate in the genre. For the first time ever, EDM finally had attracted enough people to it to justify radio stations giving it airtime. This included EDM radio stations, such as Mars FM an LA-based EDM radio station. Individuals affiliated with the station that we interviewed talked about how this helped extend the boundaries of the subculture, but Matos (2015) notes an unintended effect this had in increasing the availability of highly sophisticated and expensive state-of-the-art equipment. EDM enthusiasts were no longer simply a ragtag group of kids; they were becoming a specialized niche market and perceived as a viable business enterprise.

Outside of specialty stations, like Mars FM, most radio outlets relegated EDM to the time slots which had the fewest listeners. While the music was now starting to be accepted in some spaces, overall they were still treated with some trepidation and it would be some time before they would be treated as a legitimate music genre by "mainstream" media outlets. This mixed reception by the media represents the cultural space which EDM occupied during most of this era. Even live music spaces, for the most part, regulated EDM to nights outside of their regular schedule. Even to this day, in medium and small cities where EDM remains somewhat marginalized, the genre is regulated to weekdays in which many venues are usually closed or have a significantly low turnout.

Sociologically, the media in this phase used the EDM subculture to create a moral panic. Even when it was accepted, the music was relegated to the dark corners of otherwise unused spaces, as mainstream institutions sought to profit from, but not be seen as aligned with EDM. According to Cohen (1972), moral panics are triggered by first lobbying for action (often in the form of sensationalized media coverage), followed by a subsequent reaction by legislators and law-enforcement agencies. In this process, the media plays a crucial role, helping to promote moral panics and legitimate claims against the groups they target. Cohen (1972) also points out that the heightened media coverage can have the unintended consequence of making targeted groups more popular. In his work, he notes how this process played out among mods and rockers. According to Cohen, the media helped mods and rockers develop a greater sense of identity and group solidarity. Not surprisingly then, lurid media coverage, drew the ire and attention of public officials, also helped boost attendance at EDM events.

INTERACTION WITH OFFICIALS

Public officials, such as law-enforcement agents and politicians, faced increasing pressure from parents who were being warned by the media about the dangers their children might face at EDM events. Additionally, the media also framed law-enforcement officials as inept and incompetent in their inability to "deal with" the EDM "problem." This not only presented a political nightmare but also infuriated officials who felt they were being humiliated in the press. In many major cities, police agencies began creating task forces designed to deal with raves and other EDM events. The goal of these task forces was to shut down illegal non-licensed gatherings, under the auspices of them being a public nuisance.

Also, during this era was a renewed interest in the war on drugs. This is perhaps best explained by how then-mayor Rudy Giuliani's plan began to respond to high rates of crime in New York City, "white flight," and other issues of "urban decay." Giuliani's plan, inspired by broken windows theory, focused on increasing policing initiatives, harsh prosecution of crime, and a variety of other policies aimed at cleaning up New York City. Police raids on nightclubs were justified through the war on drugs and, as some have pointed out, unfairly targeted the LGBT+ community and racial minorities. The ultimate vision that Giuliani had was a sanitized downtown that would bring tourism to the city, increase property values, and also increase tax revenues. While scholars still debate the effectiveness of the tactics based on broken windows theory, one result was the closure of urban nightclubs in downtown New York City.

Despite ecstasy's high rate of use within nightclubs overall, it became seen as something that was most pervasive within the EDM subculture. Already criminalized in 1985, when the Drug Enforcement Agency (DEA) put it on the schedule 1 list of substances with no value for medical or research purposes—the stigma of ecstasy use would resurface as EDM events moved into nightclub spaces. Some members of the subculture that we interviewed noted that ecstasy was rarely seen in the previous era, but the move into nightclubs brought with it drug dealers who operated in those spaces. As one member recounted:

I mean in the warehouse scene [1980s–1995 the first era] sometimes you'd have people who had something on them, but it wasn't so central to the scene as some people made it out. Then when it got bigger and moved into the clubs you had dealers who worked in those clubs trying to peddle their wares [drugs] onto basically kids. A lot of those events, even those in the clubs, were all ages too . . . so they weren't old enough to drink . . . maybe they'd try something else. That's when things went a lil' sideways. (Male, 50, EDM enthusiast)

Thus, media stereotypes followed EDM enthusiasts into the clubs where outsiders to the subculture could enter and market drugs to individuals. Elsewhere, the media also blamed other drug-related crimes on EDM fans. As one respondent recalled:

Every time a vet clinic was broken into, we got the blame because they assumed some raver was stealing ketamine [a popular club drug]. If they could pin it on us they could, and sure I could see some people into the scene doing some of that but every fuckin' time? Gimmie a break. (Male, 40, Fan)

As EDM increasingly took over nightclub spaces, the media had difficulty in differentiating between the activities of the subculture on one hand and the illicit activities that sometimes occur within nightclubs. Moreover, the increasing media framing that was placed on EDM enthusiasts likely encouraged newcomers to seek out substances branded as taboo (Anderson 2009a).

Initial government information bulletins provided only loose guidelines as to how to identify EDM events, though later publications told officers what laws could be enforced to shut them down and suggested what powers to exercise based on the problem. Overall, these guidelines (see Scott 2002) suggested that officers might consider not taking any action—especially if participants weren't in any immediate danger. As one law enforcement officer I interviewed described it:

They didn't really prove a problem. The worst problem they presented was trespassing if they used an illegal venue. Then the media got involved and that's when our job got worse. Now the big wigs were involved. The chief had to put on a dog-and-pony show so that the town council would get off his case. It was so stupid. The worst we ever came up with was a couple joints and a handful of pills. If anything, it was probably more dangerous when they moved into the clubs having to deal with drunk drivers, drug dealers, and other stuff. (Male, 47, Police Lieutenant)

One promoter who had a "run in" with law enforcement explained how some local police would handle situations informally by recalling the following event:

Yeah, I was throwing this big party in Ohio. The day of the show, we are all ready to go and the cops show up. Well, here I thought, I'm screwed, I've got like 1,000 kids coming and now the party is going to be busted. The police chief took me in and told me he really didn't care what I was doing, but that he needed to cover his own butt by making me pay a fee for an event permit. I paid my fee and that was that. Apparently, one of the town council members caught wind of what we were doing, so to solve the problem and not have 1,000 kids in his town with nothing to do, he handled it this way. (Male, 51, Promoter)

Thus, in the early years, local law-enforcement agents on the ground had much more latitude in dealing with the EDM subculture. It was not until the DEA began to target EDM events in 1998 that serious action began to be taken by law enforcement (Weir 2000; Strong 2001; Yocoubian et al. 2004; Yacoubian and Wish 2006). According to Matos (2015: 250), some promoters started to hire lawyers to attend their events in case the police showed up—others that we interviewed even began taking law school courses just to understand their rights.

The peak of public officials' response to EDM came in the wake of a Drug Enforcement Administration (DEA)-initiated investigation in 1999 dubbed as Operation Rave Review, following the death of a 17-year-old girl at an EDM event in New Orleans in 1998. While classified as an ecstasy-induced dehydration, other, such as Matos (2015) have argued that dehydration at these events was a common result of participants who would dance for hours, while consuming "smart" energy drinks that contained near lethal levels of caffeine. Despite this ambiguity, the DEA alleged that the promoter of the New Orleans event, Disco Donnie Estopinal (see figure 2.1), was using European

Figure 2.1   Disco Donnie Estopinal Jr. *Source:* (Screenshot from the film *The Story of Rave Outlaw Disco Donnie* 2004).

DJs to traffic drugs, which were then sold at his events, and that venue owners were also involved as co-collaborators.

Following a short six-month investigation in which undercover agents bought illegal drugs from EDM event attendees, the DEA raided the State Palace Theater in New Orleans. While they thought they would find evidence proving their allegations, none was found. The DEA nonetheless pressed charges against Estopinal and the venue owners under laws known as "Crack House Statutes." These laws were intended to give law enforcement the power to shut down spaces which knowingly were maintained by owners whose clientele used them to sell, buy, and use drugs. The degree of misinformation put out and amplified by the media, and the highly unusual nature of Estopinol's character and events only amplified public officials' concerns of widespread drug use. Moreover, Estopinal's larger-than-life persona,[1] as well as the unconventional dress by attendees, did not help his cause. Most outsiders would have probably assumed that he was leading a cult or that it was a drug-using subculture. One Australian promoter echoed these sentiments:

> It was about really connected, getting people connected, and connecting with other people. You might not be able to hear a word they're saying, but you're connected on a totally different level. Predominantly, nightclubs were like, hey, that bitch is hot. I want to talk to her. The cops were freaking out because there would be people lined up down the block, and there would be like guys sitting massaging some other dude, another guy sitting and massaging a girl. So they're all massaging each other. This wasn't typical partying, so they assumed that there's something illegal going on, but they're not sure what it is. (Male, 45, Promoter)

Estopinal and the venue owners were indicted as co-conspirators and offered a plea agreement by prosecutors. While Estopinal held out, the venue owners relented and the charges against the promoter were eventually dropped. However, the DEA had successfully tested their ability to utilize the crack house laws to shut down rave events and could point to the result as precedent for future cases.

Despite all of this, then Senator Joe Biden proposed the RAVE Act of 2001, which proposed a widening of the 1986 crack house statute from maintaining, managing, or owning any place used to manufacture, distribute, or use drugs to include temporary or permanent uses of a premises (Cloud 2001; Eddy 2003). The new language of the bill read:

(1) knowingly open, lease, rent, use, or maintain any place, whether permanently or temporarily, for the purpose of manufacturing, distributing, or using any controlled substance;

(2) manage or control any place, whether permanently or temporarily, either as an owner, lessee, agent, employee, occupant, or mortgagee, and knowingly and intentionally rent, lease, profit from, or make available for use, with or without compensation, the place for the purpose of unlawfully manufacturing, storing, distributing, or using a controlled substance (see appendix A).

While the RAVE Act was initially overturned, largely due to its vagueness and potential for misuse and abuse, a second attempt to pass the bill was successful by placing it inside the 2003 AMBER alert bill (attached as appendix A). For rave promoters, venue owners, and other stakeholders, the message was clear: if these events were to continue, they would have to prohibit all aspects of the EDM subculture that were viewed as deviant. The strategy that many promoters turned to was to produce their events more like rock concerts, erasing references to the subculture and instituting restrictive policies to distance themselves as being part of the movement.

Passage of the RAVE Act had a chilling throughout the EDM subculture. One promoter who was charged during this period:

> After the court case in March, some of my franchises were skipped. It was about eight months where we were doing big shows. Everyone was saying when I got out, that I would be bigger than ever. But the numbers were going down. They weren't terrible, but we'd do a show where we'd normally get 3,000 and only get 1,000 if we were lucky—that's a big difference. It was a big shift. (Male, 45, Promoter)

Another major change was the pressure on EDM producers to prohibit certain items at their events. Deemed EDM contraband, these included glow sticks, pacifiers, Vicks VapoRub inhalers, bandana masks, and plush backpacks. Public officials also prohibited rooms where participants could cool off from dancing. These largely unairconditioned spaces were known as "chill out rooms." Such spaces also often provided water to individuals, which was also used as a sign that promoters were knowingly aware and promoting drug use at their events. Even if this were the case, these rooms provided a much safer environment that was now prohibited. In short, the RAVE act made EDM events less safe and also removed an important space for congregating and socializing (Hollywood 1997; Hitzler and Pfadenhauer 2002; Aherns 2013; Anderson 2014). Even today, EDM promoters have active prohibitions against many of the items listed above long after public officials' stance on them had shifted. However, as we will discuss later, these changes had much broader impacts on the subculture.

INDUSTRY PROFESSIONAL REACTIONS

Promoters have always been a kind of liaison between the outside world and the EDM subculture. This became especially true in this second era, as promoters increasingly found themselves targeted by new laws and regulations aimed at curtailing EDM events. While in the early phase of EDMs development this role was largely occupied by the DJs themselves, the separate role of promoter arose to handle the increasingly complicated task of hosting, organizing, and of course promoting EDM events. Promoters thus became the one's negotiating the price of the space, paying the artists their performance fees, and marketing the event to the public. While in the early days this was more spontaneously organized, in this phase things began to become more formal. However, to differentiate themselves these individuals often took on larger-than-life personas.

Throughout this era, promoters struggled with how to address the growing negative attention brought on by sensationalized media and later law-enforcement agencies. Initially, this meant moving into licensed spaces as an attempt to accommodate increased attendance. Moreover, they articulated love for the music, acted and participated in the larger subculture, and expressed a genuine concern for the values of PLUR. Despite their efforts to remain true to the core principles of the movement, however, a tension existed as the music became increasingly professionalized. Promoters then acted as important gatekeepers helping to decide which values were more important to the subculture and to what degree these values might be undermined in lieu of this tension.

While before the production of EDM was without many costs—venues were often unused warehouses, power was obtained through the use of generators or splicing into the electric grid, sound equipment was often donated, and other resources were obtained through an "interlocking directorate" of subculturalists, in this era promoters had to begin thinking about how to pay for their events. The move into "legitimate" venues often meant having to pay for space, security, and a variety of other elements which weren't necessary before. Some of this logic is reflected in the language promoters used to talk about organizing. Instead of focusing exclusively on the music or the political meaning of the subculture, they began talking about profits in a way that indicated they were becoming the driving force. However, like other "innovative deviants" (see Merton 1938), they used a kind of coded language and poked fun at the idea of respectability. Promoters used phrases like "making loot" [from shows], told stories of tricking major corporations into sponsoring their events (and often failing to give them credit), or engaged in other playfulness as a way to maintain legitimacy. This is all reminiscent of the early phase in which they were more of a counterculture. In short, they were trying to hold onto their original values while becoming part of the corporate music industry.

Increasingly, more and more people became aware of the profitability of EDM. Artists were also beginning to feel that they were owed a larger percentage of profits. As early as 1996, some of the earliest management companies emerged and acted as representatives for the talent performing at EDM events. Management agencies such as AM Only started off as small cottage industry-style businesses. At the 2012 EDMbiz conference, promoters recalled how this developed:

> I started off paying the DJs $150, sometimes more, and they stayed on my couch. Then the agents got involved and I had to start paying more, booking them hotel rooms, picking them up from the airport in a limo. Early on, it was underground and community driven. (Male, 40, Promoter)

The need for this was more than superficial; DJs are first and foremost artists with little to no experience managing a business. Moreover, promoters often operated as fly-by-night organizations, meaning that DJs often found themselves showing up to cities where the shows were cancelled, lacked the necessary equipment for them to perform, or were promised payment that they never received. Management companies looked out for the interests of these performers, took over the responsibility of negotiating payments, and sheltered EDM artists from the darker side of the business. Matos (2011, 2015) also points out that these early promoters were often young high school or college students who lacked financial security in the event of problems such as poor turnout or natural disasters. One promoter we interviewed spoke of his problems with his business partners:

> He [his business partner] and I ended up working together for Mardi Gras in '96. We did really well. At the time, he was letting me settle all the shows. After the Mardi Gras show in '96, he asked me to take the artist to the hotel while he settled the show. So I drive them out to some roach motel by the airport, 30 minutes out from the venue, and then it took me another 30 minutes to get back. I went to the venue and they said, "Oh, he already left." So I go to this house to find out where my cut of the money was. By the time I got back to his house, his roommate said he just left for the bus station. He had taken all the money and bought a bus ticket to Houston. I talked to him and he's like, "Oh, you know. Since I did all the work, I took the money, and I need it to start a new company in Houston." And I'm like, that's not fucking right. (Male, 40, Promoter)

Many other industry professionals had similar stories. While they recalled this era with some nostalgia, they also agreed that professionalization of the subculture was the only way it could continue to exist.

While early EDM management companies were established by music enthusiasts, they nonetheless introduced a variety of professionalizing features. Sociologically, these elements can be understood as laying the groundwork for commodification—which necessarily meant there would be some losers and some winners. One key element in this process was the introduction of legal documents that formalized the nature of EDM events. These documents were formal contract agreements with the artists. Contracts specified the amount to be paid, date of the performance, ticket prices, location of the venue, and the liability between event organizers and the artists. While in reality these contracts lacked any real penalties, especially early on due to the relatively small sums of money being risked, they symbolized and codified the arrangements in a manner foreign to original members of the subculture. Prior to this, agreements were made with a handshake and a promise, or negotiated on the back of a cocktail napkin. While it is true that a promoter of an event could be sued for violations, this rarely happened. One promoter explained:

> Well, what happened to me was, because my partner fell through, I had to pay the money back to the agencies I want to work with. But, because we have such a good relationship, and because they understand the circumstances of the situation, I'm paying it back to them out of the shows that I'm continuing to do with them. Yeah, they could lock me out, but then that would only hurt them. (Female, 45, Promoter)

One of the elements of the culture industry is the introduction of formalized rules and bureaucratic structures, and contracts played a crucial role in bureaucratizing and standardizing the event process. Additionally, as sociologist Emile Durkheim has noted (1951 [1897]), laws, rules and formal organization are signs of increasing complexity which can also mean that the subculture was struggling to maintain the bonds of the group—or in Durkheimian terms, the subculture was becoming more anomic.

One of the now retired promoters that we spoke with talked about how he proudly resisted the move into more legitimate spaces. As he explained, non-conventional spaces provided them with a blank canvas in which they could create their events. Venue owners often set limits on the design of EDM spaces, which was never a concern in abandoned warehouse spaces where even the walls could be knocked out. Using legitimate spaces meant that owners had to approve all of the elements that made the subculture unique. However, these stakeholders were often involved in how EDM events were promoted and packaged to the world, as one promoter explained:

> We found out very early on you couldn't use the word 'rave' anymore. It had negative connotations. I was trying to do a fundraiser for an AIDS charity and the executive director freaked out at me. He messaged me and asked me if this

was a rave, and at first I said no, but then later I said something like it has a rave kind of feel to it. He about lost his mind. So, I learned firsthand that rave was a four letter word. The same with the clubs too, many of them didn't want raves. (Male, 33, Promoter)

Here we can see the increasing pressure to reform the production of EDM events and the removal of the countercultural elements that might be politically threatening. As such, EDM producers increasingly tried to make their events more streamlined, or as one described it, "turn-key," to satisfy the expectations of venue owners. These standardizing elements, first described by Horkheimer and Adorno (1972 [1944]) in their seminal analysis of the culture industry also constituted one of the necessary steps toward the commodification of EDM.

DJs responded to these changes in a multitude of ways. Some resisted these changes, while others went along willingly, and competition among DJs became a frequent occurrence. This era has been described by Brewster and Broughton (1999) as the rise of the Superstar DJ. Other journalistic accounts have similarly noted that in this era DJs themselves became the star attraction. While before it never really mattered who was performing, now that was often the primary draw. Instead of being relegated to some dark corner of the dance floor, now DJs were quite literally front and center—much like at a rock concert. This brought with it aspects of celebrity that had never been part of the subculture before.

Also, while DJs and music producers initially were often the same individual, increasingly a differentiation began to occur between those who created music (music producers) and those who performed the music live. An equivalent in rock music would be whether a cover band or the original artist was performing. This meant that increasingly a DJ's ability to perform, and what they made, came to be based solely on their resumes as producers. Social relations with other members of the subculture increasingly came to be measured in terms of productivity and in relationship to the product, rather than subcultural values. As one techno DJ recalled:

At the time techno and house DJs only got booked if they produced music. That meant there was a lot more music being made, but most of it was garbage. I made a conceptual album to point this out. Also, this goes back to what we were talking about earlier. This meant less women, queer people, and other were able to get gigs. Equipment was available, but it was also expensive. There also didn't seem to be a lot of mentoring of women in the scene. (Female, DJ, Age Unknown)

As the DJ points out, this distinction also meant other differences based on race, class, gender, or sexuality were beginning to appear—the very thing that the PLUR ethos sought to escape.

During this era, major record labels also became involved and this in turn influenced how DJs thought about music. While before DJs thought of their performances as hours-long musical journeys, to fit the demands of music labels they had to produce their music within certain parameters. This included fitting the format and slicing individual songs up into three- to five-minute tracks instead of seamlessly blended mixes. In exchange, DJs received the support of a major record label, which vastly improved the quality of their music (Matos 2015). With the increased attention from public officials shutting down live performances, DJs who once made money purely from performing began to seek out new avenues through major record labels.

In this era of heightened popularity and demand for EDM, DJs also faced a variety of criticisms. Outsiders claimed that they were not "real" musicians, while insiders questioned if some DJs had strayed too far from the movement's core values. Trance DJs, in particular, were harshly criticized as catering to mass appeal rather than artistic creativity. A second criticism lodged at DJs was part of a broader societal critique that they were not "real" musicians. Many DJs responded to this criticism by composing songs that were reminiscent of classical music. One example of this is the well-known EDM producer, Tijs Michiel Verwest, better known by his stage name, DJ Tiesto. As one of the forerunners of the trance genre, one of his best-known compositions is "Adagio for Strings," which was based on the 1936 Samuel Barber orchestral composition of the same name. Other DJs faced criticism that they played pre-recorded sets, and performers like Moby that their incorporation of traditional music equipment was all part of a pre-recorded act (Matos 2015).

A third criticism that divided DJs concerned technological advances, such as the invention of turntables that played CDs. Turntables that used vinyl were heavier, and that meant DJs had to carry heavy stacks and crates of records—vinyl is if anything, not conducive to mobility. CD turntables allowed DJs to carry a wider range of material and to more easily travel to locations due to the compactness and lightweight nature of CDs. This same technology also enabled DJs to make use of file-sharing services which had become popular at the time, such as Napster. As a whole, trance DJs and producers tended to use CDs and other technological innovations more often than house DJs, who still preferred vinyl records. A 2008 post on the now defunct blulight internet message board reflects these debates:

> CD DJs I don't respect, it takes hardly no skill or effort. You could get a monkey to do it. Plus the backspins and crazy types of scratching are a laugh (like it's a toy compared to a deck) on even a top DJ CD player and can't beat that of doing the same on a technics deck, and beat matching is fairly easy. For d n b [drum and bass] it was harder but the trick was finding two tunes sounding the same

speed—that was easy as I have a good ear for that. Mixing them at the right point was slightly harder, but I used to wait until the second intro part on the vinyl had finished, then slower, bring the fader across whilst the other one was just past the first intro of the other vinyl. (Dragonxninjaxpowa 2008)

There was also a racial aspect to this debate over who is an authentic DJ. As stated above, house and techno DJs predominantly relied on vinyl records—and were among the first to establish the subculture. They also predominantly were persons of color. Trance DJs performed predominantly on CDs, and were mostly white Europeans.

By 2007, many trance DJs had reached a level of acclaim never seen before by most DJs. Popular trance DJs could play before audiences of 1,500 people or more, and were accessible to mass, mostly white, audiences. To longtime participants, trance represented everything the movement was against—conformity via harmonics, genre and form, celebrity culture, and commodification.

One way this played out was in artists' technical riders, which were growing more and more expansive. While it isn't extraordinary for DJs to make certain requests as to the technical aspects, increasingly DJs began including "artist hospitality" sections. These detailed a range of items that would be provided to the artists, such as lodging requirements, meals, liquor, and other perks. For example, one DJ requested every flavor of a particular brand of gum, another that inflatable rafts be provided, and others asked for trivial mundane items such as socks.[2] Conversely, many promoters that we talked to viewed the hospitality rider as something that could be overlooked, while others felt it was a badge of honor to deny artists items on the hospitality rider. As one female promoter explained:

> I always ignored the hospitality section because it is completely unnecessary. The hospitality rider gets longer the bigger these guys' egos get. I mean, what are they gonna do. Not play because I didn't give them the exact beer they wanted? C'mon. Also, I always felt like, as a promoter, that if I provided them everything, then they would walk all over me. (Female, 50, Promoter)

Another promoter offered up a different, yet similar, explanation to an artist's hospitality rider:

Interviewer: When I used to produce shows, I thought DJ X [actual DJ name omitted] asked for every flavor of Orbitz gum on his rider.
Respondent: You do know they're not serious with all that shit, right? It's a test to see if the promoters are reading the riders.
Interviewer: Really? They always expected me to have all that stuff.

Respondent: Right, because they were testing you. If they played with you again, you could have gotten away with asking the tour manager what they actually needed. There was a point where I asked an agent if DJ X [actual DJ name omitted] actually needed something on his rider. I think it called for "One Representative Dog." He actually laughed in my ear for like three minutes. Bastard had me stressed out trying to figure out what the hell a representative dog meant (Female, 40, Promoter).

Thus, the requests made within hospitality riders often had more to do with status, displays of power, and as a mechanism for hazing outsiders trying to become promoters. It was also a signifier to the status that these artists were given, if only by way of their own recognition.

FANS' REACTIONS

Fans were extraordinarily uneasy about many of these changes, often warning individuals that increasing commodification would jeopardize the scene. Fans would often organize protest campaigns against ongoing commodification in which they often placed the blame squarely on promoters. While the move from warehouse spaces into legitimate venues created tension between promoters and fans, legislators who drafted the RAVE Act inadvertently generated a renewed sense of solidarity among artist, fans, and promoters. In the face of government prohibitions, many began organizing and engaging in political activism to fight the RAVE Act. One such group that emerged was the Electronic Music Defense and Education Fund (EM:DEF), founded in 2001, whose purpose was:

> To raise and provide funds for legal assistance to innocent professionals in the electronic dance music business who are targeted by law enforcement in the expanding campaign against club drugs. In addition to providing funds for legal efforts to protect the industry, the EM:DEF will serve as a spokes-agency for the electronic dance music industry—providing an independent voice on behalf of industry professionals, while allowing professionals to avoid public association which could result in retaliation by law enforcement. Priority of funding of cases will be based on the following (in order):
>
> • Impact on the EDM industry's ability to remain economically viable,
> • Impact on the broader music industry's ability to remain economically viable,
> • Impact on members of the EDM community including fans and industry; and,
> • Impact on members of the broader music community including fans and industry.

The EM:DEF was founded in an effort to support the defense of three men in New Orleans who are being charged under federal crack house law. (EM:DEF 2012)

Interestingly, one of the main arguments used by the founders of the EM:DEF was based on EDM's potential as an "economically viable" business. Promoters began hosting events across the country in support of the EM:DEF, fans were encouraged to write their congresspersons, and a general feeling of activism was fostered. There was also support shown by other groups, such as the National Organization for the Reform of Marijuana Laws (NORML), who recognized that all kinds of events could be targeted under the RAVE act. These efforts aided to some degree in preserving the countercultural spirit and feelings of authenticity among many members of the EDM subculture.

However, many fans spoke rather nostalgically with us about how the mid-1990s were a confusing time period in which notions of solidarity and group identity were becoming difficult to maintain. Our respondents, like those in Anderson's (2009a, 2009b) study, also noted that, "sometimes people would just wander in that had no business being there to begin with" (Male, 36, Booking Agent). Other "outsiders" come to EDM events trying to "hook up," which was heavily frowned upon by group members. The early rave subculture prided itself on not being oversexualized, more egalitarian, and allowing for more gender fluidity among its members, but things now seemed headed in the other direction.

One way that fans coped with these changes was by utilizing new communication technologies to voice their dissent. The internet provided many EDM enthusiasts with a place in which they could communicate with artists, other fans, and promoters about issues they felt were significant. Some DJs during this period were accused of producing pre-recorded sets. An early example of this were accusations that Moby's live performances (discussed above) were "fake." A fan posted on an online mailing list that his "live keyboards" were not actually plugged into anything. Later musicians, especially trance musicians, were accused by fans of pre-recording their sets onto a CD. Regardless of the veracity of these claims, the internet provided fans with a direct line of communication with other fans and the artists themselves. They could, and many did, use it as a way to reprimand artists and other industry professionals whom they felt strayed too far from the subculture's core principles.

At the same time, the internet also broke down some barriers to entering the EDM culture, which was further aided by the shift in the kinds of venues being used. Those who became interested in EDM no longer needed cultural capital in order to gain access to the subculture, its music, or its events. EDM was now available to anyone with access to a computer. This also produced changes in the demographics of the group. The subculture, which was once dominated by African American and Latinx Gay men, was now composed of predominantly white heterosexual middle-class youth—even while they continued to utilize queer venues (Madden 2016). Early participants argued that this new crowd often had little if any connection with the subculture. These shifts were also accompanied by commodifying tendencies, as EDM events moved into licensed spaces. Status was becoming less intertwined with one's commitment to the subculture and tied more so to consumption (see Thornton 1996).

Structurally, the free spirit of the early EDM subculture was challenged by the introduction of VIP areas and other tiered tickets arrangements whereby fans could pay for special experiences. Thus, status increasingly became tied to social class and ability to pay. Malbon (1999) pointed out that this shift into legitimate spaces merged the EDM scene with what he calls club cultures. According to him, it stripped the EDM subculture of its unique substance and homogenized it into reorienting participants toward more decadent, pleasure-seeking behaviors rather than the core principles of the subculture.

CONCLUSION

Members who participated in the second era of the EDM subculture experienced a variety of changes due to internal and external pressures to become more "legitimate." During this era, members were marginalized, popularized, criminalized, and finally exonerated as they moved into more legitimate venues. This second period is perhaps best understood by Durkheim's notion of "anomie," a French word meaning, "without norms," in which group solidarity is jeopardized as social norms break down. In this study, original EDM enthusiasts were faced with questions about the subculture that they helped create and began to question the group's norms, authenticity, and what exactly it was that defined them as a movement. Event organizers no longer seemed fully committed to the values of the subculture, but instead became focused on making money. However, some promoters tried to maintain a sense of authenticity, justifying their switch to a more business-oriented model by claiming that this was the only way they could preserve the original core values of the subculture.

The concerns raised by some members of the EDM subculture point to an emerging industry framework that was promoted by the major recording companies. National tours such as the "See the Light Tour" and "Rave New World Tour" mentioned at the start of this chapter were made possible by major corporations, who organized the tours in tandem with local promoters. Thus, an emerging partnership was established which some promoters recalled, in hindsight, as an attempt by major music corporations to create a formulaic, marketable version of EDM. A few of the individuals we interviewed also noted that the major labels attempted to produce their own versions of artists and EDM events during this time period, but these were unsuccessful.

In the face of outside forces trying to commodify the subculture, some members struggled with autonomy and adherence to the group's initial core values. The result was an arrangement that, at first, kept outsiders from being

Figure 2.2 Attack of the 50-Foot Raver Zombies Flyer. *Source*: (DjMag.Com).

Figure 2.3   SupaPhat Hong Kong Phooey Twooey Flyer. *Source*: (DjMag.Com).

able to fully dominate the subculture and forced them to rely on key insiders, such as Disco Donnie Estopinal. By 2003, however, even this sort of limited autonomy was becoming difficult to maintain. Promoters were not solely to blame, as DJs also played a significant role in signing with major record labels. By altering the format of their music, hiring managers, employing booking agents to find them shows, and, most importantly, by embracing celebrity status, the DJs changed the trajectory of the subculture. Thus, while promoters played a major role in the commodification of EDM, in many ways they were also responding to the demands of the DJs and the EDM artists themselves.

NOTES

1. Estopinal was known for producing events with strange titles such as Attack of the 50 foot Raver Zombies (see figure 2.1), and Super Phat Hong Kong Phooey Twooey (see figure 2.2), and often featured psychedelic laser lights with bizarre decorations and performers (ushers in chicken costumes, a giant UFO, or a gospel choir).

2. This was based on the first author's work as a former industry insider, as well as informal conversations we had with promoters.

Chapter 3

Phase III: EDM as Culture Industry (2010–2022)

The early 2000s saw an ongoing commodification of electronic dance music (EDM), and promoters began expanding their operations to increasingly larger scales. Increasingly EDM events began to take place featuring amusement park rides, high-quality stage and lighting productions, and operating budgets in excess of $100,000. The 2003 Electric Daisy Carnival (EDC), held first in Los Angeles and then in Las Vegas after 2009, had a total operating budget of $227,250. Figure 3.1 is a profit-and-loss sheet from the event confirming this. While it does not contain the profits of the event, industry professionals we spoke with said, "We did 10k people [for the year 2003], but I'm thinking we chopped up 50-60k [in profits]." This same source went on to note that the budget in 2019 was $39 million, but would not reveal the profits made—which were presumably much higher.

In many ways the prominence of large-scale productions, like the EDC, are exemplary of the ongoing changes to the subculture. While in the second phase EDM promoters increasingly utilized "legitimate" venues, in the third era they utilized large-scale state-operated venues including sporting facilities, fair grounds, and outdoor amphitheaters. This meant negotiating with high-ranking public officials—everyone from the governor of California to local law-enforcement agencies, who began to be seen as partners and stakeholders rather than as forces to be resisted. To do so promoters increasingly had to distance themselves from the subcultural origins, and to argue that they were a vital part of city economies. Promoters increasingly traded in their neon glowsticks and plush backpacks for briefcases and suits.

As we saw in chapter 1, EDM was born out of the gay underground club scene of Chicago and Detroit. Initially, at least, the subculture was an offshoot

ELECTRIC DAISY CARNIVAL 2003
LOS ANGELES CALIFORNIA
MASTER BUDGET & PROFIT & LOSS
REVISED 6/21/03

Box Office	Capacity	Kills	Comps	Unsold		Available	Price	
$20 Ticket	0					0	$ 20.00	$
$25 Ticket	0					1,000	$ 25.00	$
$30 Ticket	0					2,000	$ 30.00	$
$35 Ticket	0					6,000	$ 35.00	$
$75 VIP Ticket	0					0	$ 75.00	$
Walkup Average	0					1,300	$ 40.00	$
Total One Show	0	0	0	0		10,300	$ 33.69	

Expenses	Budget	Revisions	Actual	Comments
01 Advertising: Print, Ads, Graphics	$ 25,000	$ 6,550	$ 18,450	
02 Backline: DJ Gear	$ -	$ -	$ -	
03 Backline: General	$ -	$ -	$ -	
04 Catering	$ 800	$ 800	$ -	
05 Electrical: Generators	$ -	$ -	$ -	
06 Fencing	$ -	$ -	$ -	
07 Fire / Medical	$ -	$ -	$ -	
08 Food/Vending/Beverage Costs	$ -	$ -	$ -	
09 Fuel	$ -	$ -	$ -	
10 Furniture: Dressing/Prod	$ -	$ -	$ -	
11 George/global	$ -	$ -	$ -	
12 Hotels: Staff	$ 1,000	$ 1,000	$ -	
13 Insomniac	$ -	$ -	$ -	
14 Insurance .00/head	$ 5,000	$ 700	$ 4,300	
15 Labor: Box Office	$ 800	$ 800	$ -	
16 Labor: Clean up crew	$ -	$ -	$ -	
17 Labor: Ken/blueprints	$ -	$ -	$ -	
18 Labor: Rigger	$ -	$ -	$ -	
19 Labor: Staff & Coordinators	$ 3,000	$ 3,000	$ -	
20 Labor: Stage Crew	$ -	$ -	$ -	
21 Lighting: Effects & Lasers	$ 2,500	$ 2,500	$ -	
22 Lighting: Screens & Projection	$ 3,000	$ 3,000	$ -	
23 Lighting: Stage Lighting/Truss	$ 8,000	$ 8,000	$ -	
24 Losses & Damages	$ -	$ -	$ -	
25 Misc. Bank Fees	$ 100	$ 40	$ 60	
26 Misc. Web Host	$ 100	$ 37	$ 63	
27 Misc. Carnival Rides	$ 25,000	$ 25,000	$ -	
28 Misc. Props/Décor	$ 5,000	$ 5,000	$ -	
29 Misc. Voicemails	$ 300	$ 95	$ 205	
30 Parking & Traffic	$ -	$ -	$ -	
31 Permits	$ -	$ -	$ -	
32 Prod. Floats, cinderblocks etc.	$ 900	$ 900	$ -	
33 Production	$ 8,000	$ 8,000	$ -	
34 Restrooms & Trash	$ -	$ -	$ -	
35 RVs	$ -	$ -	$ -	
36 Security: Police	$ -	$ -	$ -	
37 Security: Undercover	$ -	$ -	$ -	
38 Security: Yellow Jackets	$ -	$ -	$ -	
39 Sound	$ 10,000	$ 10,000	$ -	
40 Sponsor Expenses	$ -	$ -	$ -	
41 Staging	$ 4,000	$ 4,000	$ -	
42 Staging: Barricade	$ 1,000	$ 1,000	$ -	
43 Talent: Fee's, Travel & Hotels	$ 70,000	$ 63,945	$ 6,055	
44 Telephones: Line Costs	$ -	$ -	$ -	
45 Tents	$ -	$ -	$ -	
46 Trailers: Box Office	$ 450	$ 450	$ -	Schlegelmilch Trailers
47 Trailers: Dressing/Prod	$ 1,500	$ 1,500	$ -	
48 Transportation: Artists/Ground	$ 1,000	$ 1,000	$ -	
49 Transportation: Equipment	$ -	$ -	$ -	
50 Venue Rent: Variable $0/head	$ 50,300	$ 40,300	$ 10,000	
51 Walkie Talkies	$ 500	$ 500	$ -	
52 Wristbands & Passes	$ 500	$ 500	$ -	
Total Show Costs >>	$ 227,250	$ 188,117	$ 39,133	

Potential Show Ear...

Gross Receipts	$
Less: Taxes	$
Net Gross	$
Ancillary Rev.	$
Total Expenses	$

Net Show P&L>>

Ancillary Reve...

Tix Rebate	
Tix Buy S.C.	
Merch.	
Water (Gross Sales)	
Food & Bev	
Pouring Rights	
Red Bull Booth	
Moonshine Records	
Vendor Booths	
Total >>	

Additional Notes:

Figure 3.1 EDC Budget 2003. *Source*: (Twitter: @RealDiscoDonnie).

of Black and Latinx Queer culture. However, as EDM became increasingly corporatized, event promoters began to tailor their marketing initiatives to different markets and differentiated between gay raves known as circuit parties and EDM massives which catered to a mostly straight audience (Weems 2008; Weinstein 2014). This splintering into different kinds of EDM subcultures, by sexuality, happened as a slow gradual process that had a variety of implications. One promoter we interviewed had the following to say:

Everyone thought anything with a 4/4 beat and electric synthesizers was "gay" in the derogatory sense. So we preferred to use straight clubs because it was going to be a hard sell to get people to attend anyway, moving them outside of gay clubs helped shake that stigma. Now that all the artists had agents we had to get as many people as we could; we went with straight clubs. (Male, 40, Promoter)

This quote illustrates the ongoing differentiation that EDM promoters were making between circuit parties and other EDM events. As he notes, promoters chose non-gay venues to hold their events in response to a perceived stigma from outsiders. The impact of this decision, sociologically, is that it created further distance between the queer origins of the subculture and its contemporary form. This also meant that the pioneers of the music, queer men of color, were separated from mainstream EDM events as these catered to an increasingly "mainstream [white] audience." This divide between circuit parties and rave massives exists to this day (Conner 2021).

Were it not for the norms and modes of production established by promoters in the second era, these massive large-scale productions would not have been possible. Additionally, the increased size and scope of these events also meant greater and greater financial risks. This in turn led to ever-increasing fees and costs that ultimately were passed on to fans. Event organizers increasingly began to seek out and were approached by major corporations who began sponsoring their gatherings. Red Bull, Camel Cigarettes, liquor companies, car manufacturers, and major tech companies were among the early corporate sponsors of EDM events. They provided promoters with some financial security as they began experimenting with more ambitious styles of production, without being beholden to nightclub owners, who increasingly wanted a larger share of profits from EDM events.

By 2010, the EDM subculture had become a full-blown culture industry in the sense first described by Horkheimer and Adorno (1972 [1944]). The term was developed by Horkheimer and Adorno to distinguish between authentically produced popular culture and corporately produced culture. For them, the culture industry is differentiated from popular culture by an increasing tendency to mass produce culture as objectified commodities. While the origins of EDM were very much in line with the conception of popular culture, as it developed it increasingly took on more of the attributes of a culture industry. Horkheimer and Adorno identified two major features of the culture industry: standardization and pseudo-individualization. Standardization was defined by the Fordist-style production techniques and other features allowing for the mass production of culture. The term pseudo-individualization referred to the various techniques that mask the mass-produced quality of products manufactured by the culture industry and also give the illusion of uniqueness of cultural products. In a similar vein, Herbert Marcuse (1964), another Frankfurt School critical theorist, emphasized the increasing power of bureaucratic control over cultural production and consumption, another prominent feature of contemporary EDM events.

Anderson (2009a) noted this shift in her study of the alteration and decline of raves at the turn of the century. She saw EDM festivals as one format in which authentic elements of EDM culture might be preserved. Festivals resolved many of the problems faced by the move into nightclubs, including age restrictions, space for dancing, the ability to promote multiple styles of music, and dress codes. However, as we will show, the festivilization of EDM (Matos 2019), rather than promote greater innovation and artistic creativity, helped homogenize the subculture and draw it further into line with aspects of the culture industry (Conner and Katz 2019).

EDM TODAY

In the summer of 2010, three major developments took place that both exemplified and further shaped the movement into a culture industry. The first of these was the near record attendance of 185,000 fans at the EDC held in Los Angeles. This largely was due to the appearance of artists from outside the genre, such as rapper Lil' John (real name, Johnathan Mortimer Smith), and WILL.I.AM (real name William James Adam, Jr.), a member of the pop-rock group, Black Eyed Peas. More recently A List celebrities who have appeared onstage at the events include Shaquille O'Neal, Lil Nas X, Paris Hilton, Drew Carey, and other Hollywood actors and pop culture icons. As one 45-year-old DJ we interviewed said, "It wasn't that EDM became pop music, but rather pop music began to incorporate EDM, and suddenly we were popular—now the cool kids wanted to sit at our table."

The second major development that helped push EDM into a full-blown culture industry was the increasing standardization of mass-produced events. While in the second era promoters focused on locally-oriented themes, increasingly they looked toward taking their events on the road—producing EDM events across the country. One of the most well-known contemporary dance music production companies, Insomniac, took their signature event, EDC worldwide, holding several EDCs in a variety of locations, including Los Angeles, Las Vegas, Denver, Dallas, Orlando, London, and San Juan, Puerto Rico. While not all of these were successful, the Las Vegas, Orlando, and San Juan EDC events remain regular occurrences.

Insomniac also partnered with rave promoter, Disco Donnie, to produce similar events across all 50 states. After his acquittal in his FBI case, Donnie had become something of a celebrity in the eyes of EDM revelers. He is also the only promoter to have had a film produced about his experience, titled *Rave Outlaw: Disco Donnie* (Drazen 2004). His trials and tribulations at the hands of law-enforcement agents would earn him trust and allow him to enter into agreements with other EDM promoters across the 50 states—something he continues to do to this day. While the partnership between Disco Donnie and Insomniac ultimately dissolved, Insomniac continues to promote a range of other themed events regularly in Las Vegas and parts of California, and a music festival named *Electric Forest* in Rothbury, Michigan.

The third key event that helped transform EDM into a culture industry was the death of a 15-year-old girl named Sasha Rodriguez at the 2010 EDC in Los Angeles. Following her death, public officials placed a moratorium on all EDM events seeking to use publicly owned venues in Los Angeles. In the wake of this tragedy, a law was drafted, legislative proposal California AB 74, to ban EDM events in the state. In an interview with director Le Shing Liu (2019), councilwoman Fiona Ma said she was surprised to find out that banning a genre of music was unconstitutional (Romero 2011). While ultimately the bill would be ruled as unconstitutional, the moratorium on EDM events forced Insomniac to search for other places its flagship event EDC. They very quickly found a home for their 2011 EDC in Las Vegas—a destination made famous for tourism and for making illicit activities legitimate.

Despite some initial hesitation, the Las Vegas EDC turned out to be one of the most successful events hosted by the city. According to the event's website, the three-day festival attracted over 100,000 attendees. Part of the reason for the widespread and sustained success is that the city of Las Vegas built infrastructure and promoted itself as the EDM capital of the world. This strategy was so successful that, in 2013, the *New Yorker* reported that EDM nightclubs were making more revenue for resort hotels than casino gambling (Eels 2013). DJs were being paid substantial fees to perform, and nearly every casino had its own EDM club. The press dubbed Las Vegas the EDM capital of the world and went as far to say that it had eclipsed Ibiza as the top destination for EDM tourism (Feldberg 2011; Rilling 2008). While EDM promoters' reconfiguration of the Las Vegas landscape was indeed impressive, it also fully integrated EDM into the apparatus of the culture industry.

In 2011, in the wake of failed attempts to produce EDM events themselves, major corporations began soliciting the largest EDM event organizers. Companies like AEG, Live Nation, and SFX Entertainment realized that to be successful as EDM promoters, they would have to work with already established promoters. This model of colonizing existing music scenes by working through existing promoters was a strategy first enacted decades earlier when Live Nation was founded (Budnick and Baron 2011). Their founder bought out major rock promoters across the United States, realizing that, individually, promoters' profit margins were small, and the concert industry was highly volatile and risky. However, if one owned a collective of promoters, risk could be reduced and profits were potentially limitless (Budnick and Baron 2011).

Robert SFX Sillerman, who founded Live Nation, recognized that the formula he had put into play with rock music could also be applied to EDM. Sillerman realized that he was witnessing the same period of growth in EDM that he had observed earlier in rock music. With the expiration of his non-compete clause against Live Nation, he was now ready to create a new enterprise devoted to EDM. Moreover, after Disco Donnie Estopinal's acquittal (described in the previous chapter), he began partnering and working with promoters to produce EDM in cities across the United States—producing several hundred shows across the country each year. This gave Sillerman access to a pipeline of promoters ready and eager to begin producing EDM events, and allowed Estopinal to remain in control of how the events were produced. Sillerman, however didn't stop there. He went on to buy as many as 16 different companies involved in the production of EDM. Among his purchases were Beatport (an EDM file-sharing service), Flavorus (an EDM ticketing company), and Disco Productions (Estopinol's company).

On June 5, 2012, the week of the EDMbiz conference (held annually in Las Vegas one week prior to EDC), the *New York Times* ran an article announcing the deal between the two. Estopinol faced criticism from his rivals and allies, who argued that he had compromised his values in favor of profits.[1] However, as he argued on stage during a panel on the issue, this merger was necessary in order to meet the growing demands of increasing costs to produce his events. Shortly after the merger between Estopinal and Sillerman, the newly formed SFX was listed on the NASDAQ—making it the first publicly traded company devoted solely to EDM. On October 19, 2013, Sillerman stood alongside Nick Leonardus van de Wall, better known as DJ Afrojack, to ring the closing bell on Wall Street (Ross 2015). EDM had achieved an unparalleled status as a fully legitimized corporately organized culture industry. Many fans and industry insiders, however, referred to it as a symbolic death knell. Soon thereafter, other EDM companies which had resisted co-opting forces began to sell their companies to entertainment corporations, who offered them millions of dollars in cash and stock options.

EDM producers who had spent most of their youth promoting the values of PLUR, and convincing fans that they were authentically committed to the values of the scene, realized that in order for these sales to be successful they would have to convince their fanbases. Rotella, the producer of the EDC, reframed his decision to sell his company to Live Nation by calling it a "creative partnership" (Katsilometes 2013). He describes it in the following letter to his fans by stating,

In order to continue to achieve these dreams, inspire you, and produce events on a scale grander than anyone ever has, I realized that Insomniac needed to do something more and to create strategic partnerships that would continue to make it possible. For me, Insomniac is more than just a company; it's a passion that began when I was a teenager standing on street corners and handing out flyers to promote my first events. That's why I take all aspects of choosing any partner so seriously and personally.

I am pleased to announce that Insomniac and Live Nation have formed a creative partnership that will take our events to the next level. I made this choice with my heart to expand our dreams. Live Nation and their team truly respect and understand what we do and why we do it. Together we will preserve and grow the spirit of our events and our culture. This was not a decision that was based on who offered the most money, but who is the best partner.

The Insomniac team, led by myself, will maintain complete creative control of all events, just as we always have, only now we will all enjoy access to a much larger and diverse variety of venues and resources. Our ticket prices will continue to be fair and reasonable given the experience we provide and we will continue to surprise you and deliver more than we advertise. Your joy, your comfort, and your safety will always be our top priority. (Rotella 2013)

Despite such assurances as these, involvement from these companies resulted in significant changes. At events such as the EDC held in Las Vegas, for example, attendees had to utilize Ticketmaster for Insomniac's events. Over time corporate sponsorship would come to dominate the event and the types of venues used were increasingly arena style venues. One of the selling points made by the owners of EDM companies to fans was that the people who created them would stay in charge. Yet many of the originators of the subculture increasingly found themselves replaced by outsiders better suited for the increasingly corporate culture operating behind the scenes of these events.

MEDIA COVERAGE

In the previous eras, EDM was most often portrayed in an extremely negative light. As the music became more professionalized, the media coverage changed profoundly. As a recognized legitimate business enterprise, the media began to cover EDM in a far more positive light. Before the widespread colonization and corporatization by outsiders, EDM was seen as a wasteful nonproductive use of time. Once money began to flow from wealthy business investors, and the music was recognized as something that could be profited from (mostly via tourism), the media began to report on EDM's positive role, especially in economic growth. Artistic excellence, if reported on at all, was a secondary consideration in media accounts. EDM promoters, DJs, and other industry professionals are still to this day regularly featured in national news publications (*Wall Street Journal*, *Forbes*, *Rolling Stone*, and *Billboard*) and on billboards along the Las Vegas strip. While some negative press persists, it is now marginal—gone are the days of sensationalized headlines and constant moral panics about EDM's role in corrupting youth.

While, in the second era, the media only inadvertently played a role in popularizing EDM, now their role was intentional. Ignoring all countercultural aspects of the original EDM subculture, the genre now receives enormous popular publicity. EDM promoters prominently advertise the precautions they take to minimize any deviant activity and highlight their ties with public officials (see figure 3.2). In this way, EDM event organizers utilize many of the tactics employed by public relations departments of Fortune 500 companies. As some scholars have noted, this depoliticization and mass marketing of cultural phenomenon represents the Disneyfication of EDM (see Bryman 1999; Conner and Katz 2019). Indeed, many EDM organizers utilize outside public-relations specialists and other experts to maximize their advertising expenses and to boost positive perception of their companies. In the case of EDC, the promoters made significant use of economic impact studies that provided them with data journalists could use to sell papers. Press releases and headlines in major newspapers began to read "How Music

Figure 3.2   Pasquale Rotella and Clark County Commissioner and Chairman of the Board Recognizing EDC's Five-Year Anniversary. *Source*: (Las Vegas News Bureau).

Festivals Pump Billions into the US Economy" or "Electric Daisy Carnival Brings $207 Million to Las Vegas' Economy" (Coates and Humphreys 2008; Beacon Economics 2012; Domanick 2012; Powell 2012; Prevatt 2014; Shah 2015). Just as Cohen (1972) observed in his theory of moral panics, the media now plays a significant role in the unmaking of the panic. Here we can see the media's shift from hysteria designed to enrage the public, to promoting a spectacle of consumption (Epstein 1994; Murji 1998; Heir 2002; Hill 2002; Rosenbaum 2002).

INTERACTION WITH OFFICIALS

Not surprisingly, changes in the way the media portrayed EDM also coincides with how public officials (politicians and law enforcement) interact with those within the subculture. Today, EDM promoters and fans appear not in handcuffs, but rather shaking hands with politicians and law enforcement (see figure 3.3). Many event organizers now use state-owned venues such as parks, fairgrounds, and coliseums and market their events as EDM festivals—not as "raves," which carries a social stigma from EDM's past

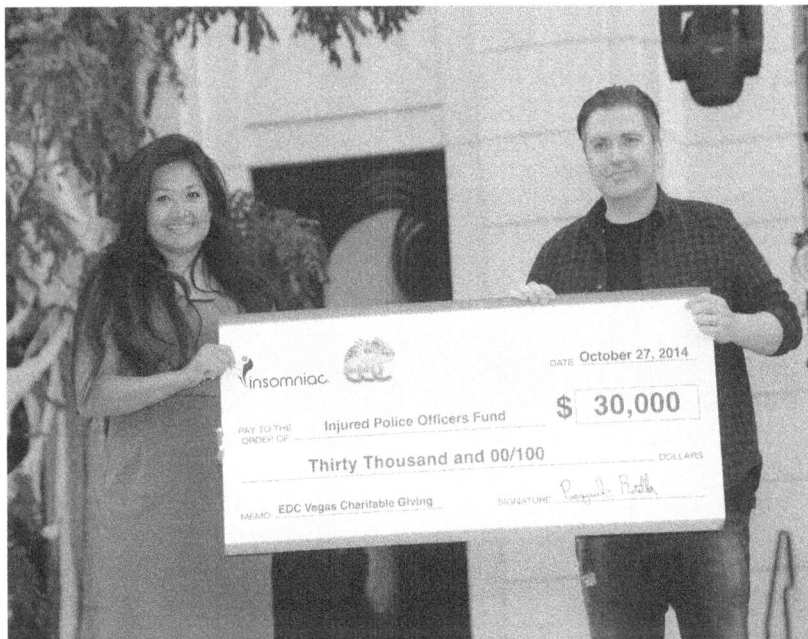

Figure 3.3   Pasquale Rotella Making a Donation to the Las Vegas Police Department. *Source*: (Las Vegas News Bureau).

that promoters want to avoid. They also promote the increasingly popular, if not widely criticized, notion that investing in cultural amenities attracts a more highly educated population, which in turn helps bring jobs and infrastructure (Florida 2009). As mentioned above, many of the top EDM promoters work with consulting firms to conduct economic impact studies to produce data backing up these arguments. While events like EDC undoubtedly have a positive impact, in reality many of the jobs created by these events are low wage, short-term positions. Additionally, no one has pointed out the environmental impact that holding an event, like EDC, which generates a significant amount of waste. While some festival organizers have incentivized attendees collecting their own trash and properly disposing of it, this appears to be an effort to deflect from the actual environmental strain produced by their events.

Due to the size of EDM festivals, elected city officials are now part of the organizing strategy, if for no other reason than because these events are organized in tax-funded state-managed facilities like the Las Vegas Motor Speedway. Police, who were once the enemy of EDM enthusiasts, are now employed to patrol, in uniform, around the festival grounds to ensure the safety of attendees. This has also sometimes placed the organizers of these events at odds with their attendees, as the police have some discretionary power in these situations. While conducting observations at EDC from 2010–2015, we observed arrests being made for a variety of infractions— from "dancing too hard," trying to pass off counterfeit tickets, and for drug possession and use.

Public officials have called on promoters to respond to a variety of these issues, and the main concerns raised seem to be illicit drug use—several felony arrests for drug possession are made at EDC each year, usually fewer than 10 DUI charges and hundreds of misdemeanor offenses. The response by many promoters to mitigate some of this has come in the form of drug-amnesty bins placed at entrances, alongside public-service announcement videos played at the festival entrance warning attendees of the potential dangers of drug use. More recently, law-enforcement agencies also have begun to employ drone technology to look for any instances of illegal activity. While the justification is often that it is to stop a mass terrorism event, a valid concern, there is little transparency as to other crimes that drones might be used to detect. Rather than resist public officials attempts to monitor these events, the organizers' role is to promote the acceptance of these changes among their attendees—and deflect any dissent. Thus, whereas promoters of early EDM events actively resisted law enforcement, today they have become incorporated into new systems of control—and are also implicated in the continued war on drugs.

INDUSTRY PROFESSIONAL REACTIONS

While the incorporation of EDM as part of city planning indeed marked a significant shift, there were also several other important developments that allowed the culture to become popular. Within the music, and among the musicians themselves, this was reflected in the increased involvement of major record labels and the incorporation of pop music (Bentley et al. 2014). As one commercial DJ we interviewed explained:

> It's not that I've changed what I do. I'm a top 40 DJ. But, something happened. EDM became pop music, and pop music became EDM. The two learned from each other and changed. I still play top 40, it's just that top 40 is now EDM. (Male, 35, DJ)

One example of this is in mainstream music artists who began sampling and remaking popular EDM tracks, like Kanye West's use of Daft Punk's "Harder, Better, Faster, Stronger" in 2007. Daft Punk, a DJ duo featuring Thomas Bangalter and Guy-Manuel de Homem-Christo, was known for their signature space-age costumes complete with face-obscuring helmets— a critique of the celebrity culture they saw invading EDM culture, which ironically helped them gain popularity. The duo also was hired to produce the soundtrack, and appear in, the 2010 sequel to the 1982 film, *Tron*—titled *Tron Legacy*.

Other EDM artists, such as Adam Richards Wild, known as DJ Calvin Harris, also began working alongside major pop icons. Harris's collaboration on the song "We Found Love," with pop singer Robyn Rihanna Fenty, better known as Rihanna, became the longest-running number-one single of 2011. Even more significant was longtime EDM veteran David Guetta's collaboration with the pop group, Black Eyed Peas. Together they produced the song, "I Got A Feeling," which, in 2009, became the best-selling song in iTunes history. Even Madonna jumped on the EDM bandwagon, with her 2012 release of MDNA (a clever play on MDMA, the chemical name for ecstasy), a pop style EDM album. She also was invited to introduce EDM artist Avicii at the Winter Music Conference (Sager 2012). The peak of the merger with mainstream music and EDM came in 2014 when EDM artists were nominated and *performed* at the Grammy Awards ceremony.

While EDM artists had been involved with the Grammy's since 1999, with Frankie Knuckles winning best re-mixer of the year award, they were largely obscure figures. The category of Best Electronic/Dance Album was established in 2005, changed to Best Dance/Electronica Album, and then in 2015 changed again to the Best Dance/Electronic Album. While to outsiders this may seem trivial, but these categories determine the pool of artists eligible to enter. The change to Best Dance/Electronica album, for example, allowed for a broader pool of artists to be nominated, with Madonna winning the award in 2007 for her EDM-inspired pop album *Confessions on a Dance Floor*. The award in 2010 went to pop star Lady Gaga, also inspired by EDM. As one industry insider we interviewed told us: "Electronica was a term we in the music industry created. We wanted to help artists in the pop world cross-over and vice versa. Most people don't know the difference between house, techno, psytrance, IDM, EDM but they did know music that was created with electronics, and if you're trying to move albums making it accessible is key" (Female, 54, Music Marking Professional). The shift in 2015 made it clear that the award wasn't necessarily meant solely for artists catering to fans of EDM. However, as the earlier quote suggests, EDM was becoming so popular that these lines were blurry as EDM was becoming more like pop music.

DJs themselves began to engage in a form of self-criticism, responding to both fans and colleagues alike that the music they were producing was becoming overly formulaic. One of the most public criticisms came in the form of a EDM song written by the group, DJs From Mars. Their hit, "Fat Ass Drop," criticized the formulaic construction of EDM music. Specifically, their song broke down the basic structure of many of the top EDM songs. According to the lyrics, "Just follow the instructions and you'll be an electronic music producer in no time . . ." and ends with "Now create a Facebook page and post this crap" (DJs From Mars, 2013). As the song suggests, there were increasingly formulaic ways in which DJs constructed and marketed their musical compositions.[2] However, DJs in the second era that we spoke with talked about the importance of "reading a room." For them, this meant being able to shift one's performance to accommodate the specific musical tastes of the crowd for whom they were performing. They articulated this as a feedback loop between audience and performer. In the context of large-scale festivals, this wasn't necessarily the case. More importantly, DJs felt they were competing with other acts to create the most audience engagement. Even Pasquale Rotella, promoter for EDC, noted this by commenting that, "Last year . . . you would hear, no joke, some of the same tracks on the biggest stage eight or ten times" (Bain, 2013).

With artistic creativity stifled to conform to the presence of audience expectations, DJs began to distinguish or "pseudo-individualize" themselves through other means. One way they attempted to achieve this was through their stage performances. As in the case of Deadmau5 (real name, Joel Zimmerman), who performs while wearing a mouse helmet (see figure 3.4). Others however, opted to dazzle their audiences through the use of massive laser light shows, fireworks and other pyrotechnics, dance troupes, animated projections produced on LED screens, or wearing wild costumes.

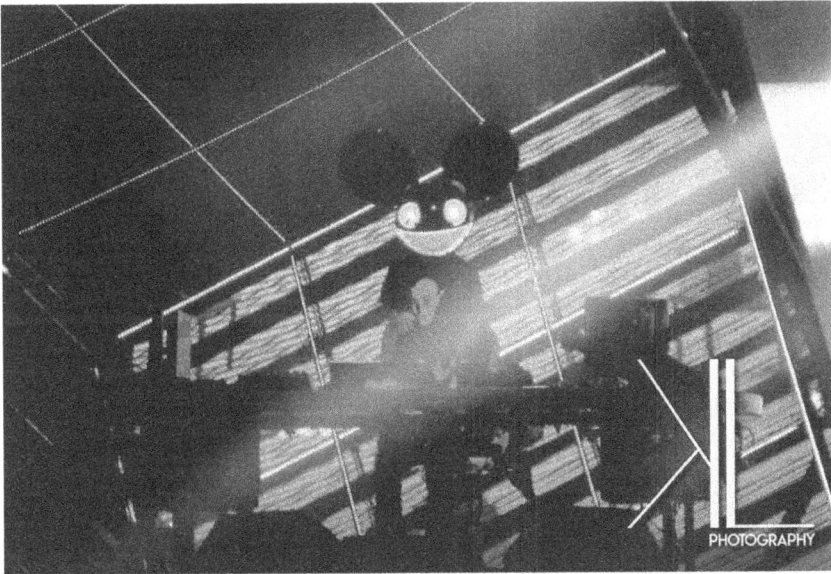

Figure 3.4 Deadmau5 in His Signature Mouse Helmet. *Source*: (Kate Morgenstern, ndk8media.com).

DJs, promoters, and other industry professionals all confessed at the EDMbiz conference, and to me in interviews, that this shift was motivated by the fact that the modern EDM DJ is uninteresting to look at. This was echoed in interviews with top producing DJs such as Deadmau5:

I just roll up with a laptop and a midi controller and "select" tracks and hit a spacebar. Ableton [a DJ program used in live performances] syncs the shit up for me . . . so no beat matching [or] skill [is] required. "Beat matching" isn't even a fucking skill, as far as I'm concerned anyway. So what, you can count to 4. Cool. I had that skill down when I was 3, so don't give me that argument, please . . . .

My "skills" and other PRODUCERS skills shine where it needs to shine . . . in the goddamned studio, and on the fucking releases. That's what counts. . . because this whole big "EDM" is taking over fad, I'm not going to let it go thinking that people assume there's a guy on a laptop up there producing new original tracks on the fly. Because none of the "top DJs in the world" to my knowledge have. Myself included.

You know what makes the EDM show the crazy amazing show that it is? You guys do, the fans, the people who came to appreciate the music, the lights, all the other people who came; we just facilitate the means and the pretty lights and the draw of more awesome people like you by our studio productions. Which is exactly what it is. But to stand up and say you're doing something special outside of a studio environment when you're not just plain fuckin' annoys me. (Zimmerman 2012)

The attitude reflected by this artist highlights the pressures and conflicts among EDM artists themselves. As he notes, new technologies were emerging that made specialized knowledge about how to DJ obsolete. Zimmerman, a relative newcomer to the world of EDM in 2012, is lashing out at DJs who were critical of those using these new technologies and also defending himself against criticisms of his authenticity to the subculture. However, these comments gloss over the fact that he himself became a celebrity DJ due to his stage name (Deadmau5) and costumes. His quote also illustrates the relative limits to which DJs can differentiate themselves from each other, by placing the emphasis on the larger-than-life features dominating EDM festivals.

While some DJs have today accumulated massive fortunes, prompting *Forbes* magazine to create a listing of the top earning DJs on their website in 2012 (Greenburg 2012), those who lack the backing of major labels talked with me about being increasingly marginalized. These DJs refer to themselves as the DJ middle class, or as "just a club DJ." A panelist at the EDMbiz 2011 conference consisting of EDM professionals talked about this change:

> You go back 10 years, 12 years, 15 years. DJs created their identity solely on what they were doing as DJs. What they were playing, because they were playing records other guys didn't have. Now the model is, all music is available to everyone immediately. So what sets people apart now more than it was then is the records they are producing and how the record is attached to a lot of what the panel before was talking about. So that's the paradigm shift—identifying artists who were extremely creative DJs versus producers who are doing cutting edge things. There are a lot of producers succeeding and then wanting to transition to live performance.
>
> The era of a DJ just strictly playing tracks in a club and curating the music is over. With DJs, you're not going to find one that's strictly producer based. This is because the press is not going to follow someone unless they have a record to promote. Going back in time to 15 years ago, this wasn't the case. (Male, age unknown, EDM Journalist)

Another EDM professional was very candid with us about this during a personal interview:

> All of these guys talking about peace and love and all that bullshit, it's not. If we're not careful, they will choke it off. This was a rule that was broken in underground and in clubs. They're choking that aspect of it off. Where are

warehouse parties now? So okay, we'll do a warehouse party. Then these DJs come in with festival riders, and now it's not an underground show anymore. The cost to build these venues is tremendous, so now you try to do a warehouse show where it used to be $5 to get in; and now you've got to charge $75! The essence of what a warehouse underground party is about, it's not, it's bullshit. Corporate sponsorship is fine if it helps keep the cost of tickets down; they have a method to their madness. The margin is getting smaller and smaller. The room for error is smaller and smaller. Now you have a situation where it's sort of, when you hear about the economy and there's no middle class anymore, I'm starting to see it. (Male, 50, Venue Owner)

Being a DJ who consistently receives bookings now means having the backing of a major record label, which provides sophisticated equipment and helps in producing original music. The notion that DJs are curators of music, tastemakers, or that they provide some other function beyond producing music and touring has changed. Instead, they are now measured by their revenue-producing capacity. Thus, the truly innovative DJs have been marginalized, and with their traditional outlets being commodified, the DJ's role had become another link in the culture industry's production chain.

Part of the allure of EDM events was in event organizers' and promoters' ability to create a stimulating otherworldly environment. Promoters that we interviewed noted that early on this took the form of utilizing sound systems that would allow participants to "feel" the sound via utilization of laser lights and other spectacular features. The most successful EDM promoters were those which combined different forms of entertainment and theatrics—ranging from sword swallowing, gospel choirs, and even satanic imagery to captivate audiences. However, due largely to legislative constraints from the RAVE Act, promoters were increasingly being forced to tone down some of the more sensational aspects of their events.

Once EDM events began to be marketed to more mainstream audiences, many of these spectacular elements started to reappear. EDM promoters who we talked with and heard speak at music conferences discussed organizing their events as "experiences." Framing EDM events as experiences was also a way that organizers tried to claim a connection with earlier incarnations of these events. The term "experience" referred to the various non-musical aspects of their shows including carnival rides (see figure 3.5), interactive artwork, and performers who circulated throughout the event providing a sense of spontaneity (see figure 3.6). However, they also went to great lengths in order to create opportunities for fans to interact with one another in meaningful ways. EDC, for example, has a wedding chapel for individuals to get married and a variety of spaces specifically set up for photo opportunities.

Figure 3.5   Carnival Rides and Art Installations at EDC Las Vegas. *Source*: (Las Vegas New Bureau).

Figure 3.6   Art Car. *Source*: (Las Vegas New Bureau).

While these kinds of spectacular images have always been present within EDM, in this third era these features began to eclipse the artistic elements. Moreover, corporate sponsorship increasingly began to be part of this. For instance, Red Bull, at the 2010 EDC, brought skydivers, who were illuminated by pyrotechnic sparklers strapped to their feet and could be seen slowly descending in the nighttime desert skyline. At the 2014 and 2016 EDC a large stage was sponsored by 7UP, complete with their logo and lime green lights which washed over those in front of the stage (see figure 3.7). Additionally, corporate sponsorship of EDM performers during the week leading up to EDC can be seen up and down the Las Vegas strip.

In earlier times EDM promoters went to great lengths to ensure that these kinds of theatrics were unique, but in this era there is a continuous recycling of previously seen concepts and ideas. However, promoters also appropriated these kinds of non-musical features, stage designs, and auxiliary elements from other large festivals such as Burning Man, Coachella, and many others. As one of the staff of a major EDM festival told us in an interview: "Oh yea, we go to Burning Man every year to network with different artists that we can get. There's a lot of promoters that go there to poach ideas. If you see it at Burning Man there is 90% probability you're going to see it at a music festival not soon after . . . and if you haven't seen it at a music festival

Figure 3.7 7Up Sponsored State at EDC 2015. *Source:* (Kent Otto, ElectronicMidwest .com).

yet, just wait, you will" (Male, 30, Event Organizer). Another reason for the increasing similarity across EDM events and large-scale music festivals is because of the limited number of companies capable of designing stages that can meet the demands of these large-scale events. While promoters came up with the various designs, the behind-the-scenes work was done by third parties who worked with various festival producers. According to those involved in the planning and production of EDM events in 2012, only four companies existed that could produce the stages required by these massive spectacles.

These non-musical aspects are designed to create feelings of authenticity and spontaneity at large-scale massive EDM events. However, as these elements become more complex, there is an increased need for greater bureaucratic and technocratic control. Without the proper staff and professionals, these elements can quickly go from being awe-inspiring to disastrous. Thus, EDM events, which had already started to be reconfigured by outsiders, were increasingly becoming more scripted like rock music festivals. At the EDC this included highly specialized individuals who coordinated with performers via short-range radios so that pyrotechnics, lighting, and sound were synchronized in unison to create an all-encompassing sensory experience. Even within nightclubs where EDM artist perform, there are often highly elaborate productions that are specifically timed at predetermined intervals (Mears 2020). This is more than mere conjecture. The 2014 and 2015 EDMbiz conference, organized by the promoters of EDC, had entire panels of seasoned professionals discussing how to create an experience that is similar for every participant:

> When we plan, we try to think five years ahead. The idea is that we develop a theme that we are going to stick with for some time. We also consider how much can be reused at different events. (Male, 45, Promoter)

So, while EDM organizers continuously sought out ways to make their events more "innovative" and "interactive," they also increasingly made their events more bureaucratically organized. At the 2010 EDC, event organizers provided an incredibly elaborate list of more than 50 rules of "do's" and "don't's" for attendees to follow.

As in the second phase, where major music industry professionals became more involved, in this phase other types of business professionals appeared. These included not only some involved with the music business but also others who specialized in other aspects. One accountant we met at the EDMbiz 2014, explained how he used his professional knowledge to assist EDM performers in maximizing their profits and minimizing their tax liability:

So what I do is set up different shell corporations to handle the different aspects of DJs. One corporation might handle a DJ's live performance, another handles their broadcasting rights, and I've set up some to handle the licensing rights of their image. So one thing we do is when a DJ's image is used on the flyer, one of the corporations will sell the image to another company; that way, there is something happening on paper. I also take care of their visas so they can come over. If they create businesses here, they can also become citizens. When you get into being an international DJ, it is really complicated. Since they are dealing with so much money, they also have to get creative in how things are set up. My firm only handles three DJs total because it is so much work. (Male, 25, Industry Professional)

Indeed, the EDMbiz conferences seemed to be dominated by individuals, such as the one above, who were seeking ways in which they could enrich themselves off of the culture without any concern for preserving it. The presence of these outside industry professionals, whether intentional or not, shifted the way DJs, promoters, and even longtime participants of the subculture talked about EDM. In short, the conversations that we observed at the EDM business conference focused almost solely on profitability and very few on artistic innovation or creativity.

At the 2014 EDMbiz conference, only one booth out of thirty was focused on anything outside of profitability. The vast majority were focused on some commodifiable aspect of EDM. The one outlier at the event was devoted to creating awareness of the environmental footprint of music festivals (trash, electricity, and other issues of environmental sustainability), and in maintaining the cultural ideals that were once expressed as PLUR (Peace, Love, Unity, Respect). This group, however, seemed highly out of place amid those vendors competing for the business of festival and event producers, DJs looking for ways they could become noticed, and recent college graduates wanting to work in the business. They were marginalized, ignored, and even scoffed at by this newer breed of industry insiders.

Given all of these changes, it is perhaps not a coincidence that EDM festivals themselves became opulent affairs—featuring unparalleled stage productions. The 2014 EDC event stage was reportedly the largest stage ever assembled in North America. One EDM fan site put this into perspective saying:

EDC Las Vegas welcomed high standards leading up to Insomniac's annual highlight festival, particularly directed towards their main stage. The production team definitely didn't disappoint. The "Kinetic Cathedral" located at the "Kinetic Field" was the largest stage ever constructed in North America. Let's put it into perspective:

The stage was 440 feet long. That's 147 yards which is 27 yards longer than a football field: Goal post to goal post. Almost 6 times larger than the stage used during Pink Floyd's "The Wall" tour, and more than double U2's 360 tour stage that held the previous record.

Just shy of 80 feet tall, this stage was roughly the size of a 7-floor building. If there was a single flight of stairs going to the top of the stage, it would have about 140 steps.

The Cathedral also featured 28 LED displays, 1,000 light fixtures, 30 lasers, and required 2.5 million watts of power to function. (EDM Sauce 2014)

Amid this spectacular stage design, DJs were swallowed whole by walls of LED lights and lasers. DJs were, however, less worried about notions of artistic excellence and more concerned with the visual and aesthetic aspects of their performance. Many of those in attendance that we spoke with informally, couldn't even name the acts they were watching. While the festival experience has become the preferred site for top producing DJs, for many older fans the festival lacked the intimacy that drew them to the subculture. One industry professional, a promoter and nightclub owner, had the following observation:

I also think there are a lot of false fronts in the business these days. A lot of people wrestling for control. Is it good to have 3 people calling all the shots? That's dangerous as well. When it comes down to the money, all of these individuals, kids doing freefall things, it's more difficult for them. They can't get talent. There's a festival, all this festivity, and DJs can't play anymore for 6 months anywhere, and you do a big festival, it really hurts. So many facets of the festivals. Tommy Trash is playing Electric Zoo, and he can't play a club. And you like Tommy Trash . . . you want to see him in a club where you can connect and be there. You go to a festival, you may be a quarter of a mile from the stage. So how does that help Tommy Trash develop? But he'll probably get paid more to do a festival. And then the agents kowtow to the bigger festivals, because that helps make the DJs get more money and it's this vicious cycle . . . I brought that up last year. I brought it up on the panel, closing comments. And they cut my mic off. It's just suffocating and now what we're starting to see is several of these $40-50,000 DJs now have completely lost their identities because they're not playing at the clubs. They're not exclusive now. And these festivals now with 80,000 tickets, you don't know who's actually bringing in the people. So now they're in shows and not selling tickets. Your fan bases are deteriorating rapidly if you're not a superstar, and there's only a handful of superstars. That's what everybody is ignoring, that fact, because they don't want to, you know. That's something you should include because . . . why would you make it so your fans can't see you 6 months out of the year? Why are you doing that if you care? It's bullshit. (Male, 50, Club Owner)

FANS' REACTIONS

Amid the dizzying spectacular displays at contemporary EDM music festivals, the fans have focused less on dancing and more on the visual stimuli—giant screens, laser light shows, fireworks, and visual spectacles—at EDM events. Attendees huddle together trying to get close to the stage like at any other rock concert, hoping for a chance to gain a glimpse of their favorite EDM performer. This represents a stark contrast to the original subculture, which was specifically organized around dancing. As one participant reflected, "These days people just stand in front of the stage. Back in the old days people didn't stand around . . . THEY DANCED!" (Female, 45, DJ). The way attendees "consume" these massive EDM events are without a doubt the result of the reconfiguration of them to emphasize their spectacular, aesthetic qualities; however, it's important to remember that those changes were the result of promoters seeking to attract mainstream audiences.

Fans of EDM today may generally be divided into two groups: those who are usually but not always older and still embrace the values of PLUR which defined the original rave subculture, and those who are either unaware or uninterested, if not downright hostile to, these countercultural values. This latter group greatly outnumbers the older, former rave enthusiasts. The older, longtime participants in the EDM subculture are critical of what they see as the encroachment of corporate forces. One of the issues they feel particularly strong about is the increasing presence of outsiders. As one fan-turned investigative journalist wrote:

> Meanwhile, the mainstreaming of electronic dance music has ensured that a once tight-knit underground community has been replaced by hordes of agro fans who didn't realize that artists like Swedish House Mafia and Avicii are directly descended from the old school house of Detroit and Chicago. (Bain 2013)

These longtime fans see the younger generation as participating in a subculture whose history they do not understand. Another journalist observed the way in which these changes were reflected in the demographics of who attended EDM events:

> Amazingly, EDM has discovered how to sell itself to straight, white, American teenage boys. The very same lot that, had they lived decades earlier, might have been burning disco music in Comiskey Park. This time around, unmistakably, the movement is fronted largely by white guys, and you'd be hard pressed to find any gay subtext, aside from the shirtless bros bumping into each other in the crowds. (Munzenrieder 2013)

The above quote also points out the irony that such popularity has marginalized many of those responsible for creating the EDM subculture, while attracting others who are openly hostile to the original values of the group. However, many newer fans are simply uninformed about the history of EDM. We spoke with one such individual:

> Before attending EDC, I didn't even know a culture existed. Then when I came here, I was really happy to find out that there was a whole community and culture behind the music. (Female, 22, Fan)

Some older fans have tried to reach out to these persons. However, they feel that their efforts are undermined by the nature and magnitude of contemporary EDM events.

Often fans explained to us that what was at stake for them was not only remembering the history of the music but also the very essence of the subculture itself. They talked about the erosion of the values, beliefs, and rituals that had distinguished them as a subculture of like-minded individuals. They spoke of feeling a loss of the connection with other participants that once was the main focus of EDM events, and talked about the change in how individuals treated and connected with one another, as in the following passage:

> The tone of MW-Raves, says Labocitch, "was very collegial. People were giving each other rides to parties and helping people out. You could be a 16-year-old kid and say, 'Hey, can somebody pick me up from my parents' house?' And somebody would drive out, pick you up from your parents' house, take you to a party, and return you. There were no thoughts like, "Something bad's going to happen to me." (Matos 2015)

A 2012 newspaper article amplified this sentiment

> This thinking harkened back to my early days in New York in the early 2000's, the time when I went out to clubs the most and enjoyed myself the least, always wondering how everyone knew each other and what it felt to be liked and have a great time. In a crowd, the feeling of isolation has long felt like home to me. I'm a lot less awkward and self-conscious than I used to be, but it strikes me that the profound aloneness I felt as a result of my self-imposed isolation at EDC was a very similar emotional experience to how I've always felt in big groups where there is dance music playing. This is why I usually enjoy dance music all by myself through headphones. It's been that way since I was 12, jamming solo to Black Box and C+C Music Factory. And it's still often that way. The world is engaging with dance music on hugely visible levels, but even when I'm listening to and loving the same Top 40 pop trash as everyone else, I'm doing it alone with my iPod at the gym or on the subway. The illusion of unity is offered, but

inessential. Until, that is, you find yourself in a crowd, confronted by just how alone you are.

I know I could have penetrated the crowd and turned on the charm just for the sake of socialization. I interviewed people on VH1 reality shows for years—I can talk to anyone. But what was the point in making friends for a few hours, or a few days? With 20-year-olds? Why bother? To make the MDMA-kissed equivalent of camp friends that I'd get to see when we did it all over again next year? (Juzwiak 2012)

Similarly, others we spoke with talked about how the notions of PLUR were being lost. As one anonymous blogger posted to an EDM group:

What is happening to our community? It's become so negative and is revolving around trends. What happened to loving and uplifting one another? Can we take a step back and really remember what raves are about? [PLUR is] certainly not about drugs or your outfit. It's about uniting with like-minded people; people uplifting one another. Loving one another. Coming together to forget all the negativity in the rest of the world. Where we hug each other and smile, exchange kandi, and give a tiny piece of our hearts to a complete stranger. C'mon. Let's bring back PLUR. (Female, 25, EDM Fan)

These fans were also critical of large-scale nature of contemporary EDM events. An article in the *Guardian* captured this spirit:

The increasingly bread-head and circus-like aspects of EDM have provoked a backlash from those who feel dance culture is swapping underground intimacy in favor of soul-less bombast that stuns and stupefies audiences into slack-jawed submission. The *Wall Street Journal*, of all places, recently railed against, "The Dumbing Down of Electronic Dance Music." Long time west coast rave watcher Dennis Romero penned a caustic verdict for *LA Weekly* on this June's Vegas EDC: "A press-play parade of millionaires going through the motions." Dance Safe's Messer, a veteran of the idealistic PLUR (peace, love, unity, respect) oriented rave underground of the 90's, complains that the dance festivals offer a "packaged, containerized experience...these events are all about raging hard, getting as fucked up as you can. Not necessarily even about dancing, just being a face in this giant extravaganza." (Reynolds 2012)

The above quote also exemplifies older fans' displeasure with not being able to dance because of the large crowds and the physical layout of the new events. Moreover, many older dance music enthusiasts feel self-conscious in the face of outsiders not committed to the values of the subculture. Finally, older fans expressed frustration with how newer fans used the notion of PLUR to justify what they saw as excessive drug and alcohol use. Many also noted that the huge crowds, tightly packed venues, and lack of access to water actually made these events less safe both for those using and not using drugs.

Older participants described newer male fans as part of what they derisively referred to as the "bro' culture." A recent blog post by Saraceno (2013), an EDM enthusiast, both depicts with a photo (see figure 3.8) and describes at length the problematic nature of bro' culture in the eyes of long-term fans:

> It's also the purveyor of cultural ideals that stand in direct conflict with rave culture's ideals. New York is about getting things done with a purpose. New York is not about nonchalantly stumbling upon someone or something to help or assist. It's about me, me, me (and my money, my job, my things).
>
> For the East Coast, EDM events like EZoo are not cultural harbingers of a changing tide in post-Millennium culture. Rather, they are little white suburban meccas for frat boys to take lethal doses of MDMA. They can't be anything more because the dominant culture prevents it. It doesn't play well with the current mindset.
>
> For proof, imagine presenting the idea of there being some greater rave-type EDM-culture forming in today's youth generations to a New Yorker. "Do you think today's youth are becoming more connected, more concerned with one another's wellbeing, and do you think it has something to do with EDM culture?" The idea would be dismissed as "hippy-dippy shit" as they'd exit the conversation to check their email or grab a delicious bagel.

Figure 3.8   Example of a Bro. *Source:* (Las Vegas News Bureau).

Seeing events like EZoo where you have 23 Syracuse frat bros getting bussed in to do "molly" and finance guys getting together to ditch the suit. (Saraceno 2013)

While some might argue that this is a stereotyped image of what bro culture looks like, it was also a label that some of these individuals embraced. We met several fans who used the term to refer to themselves and their friends, emphasizing their masculinized, sexist self-image and young women who were new to EDM culture and dressed provocatively were labeled "Prostitots":

Besides, turn of the 2012s festivals have far more beefed up security than raves ever did. Also, "rave" connotes baggy pants and oversized T-shirts; "EDM festival" connotes hot pants and pasties. Those, combined with fairy wings (a perennial), came, says Rotella, "from people trying to replicate our flyers. My old flyers encouraged people to dress up. We wouldn't encourage them to dress naked." But many did. "Prostitots, we call them here—girls who dress up like prostitutes, who go to the events in just their bra and underwear," says Bonnie Chuen. The look took hold about the same time EDC went to L.A. Coliseum— as social media took over. "It's the Flickr effect," says Glazer. "My theory is, it was four girls the first year; the next year, a hundred; then a hundred became a thousand. (cited in Matos 2015: 354-355)

An example of a group of prostitots is pictured below (figure 3.9). These young women are sometimes described as the female members of the bro culture and are similarly criticized. One EDM promoter attempted to ban this kind of dress at his events, to no avail. Older fans we spoke with criticized the bro's and prostitots for their lack of knowledge about EDM culture, their over-concern with their body, excessive use of drugs and alcohol, refusal to treat others with respect, and their resistance to other fans who were trying to educate them about the group's values. Some trace the emergence of bro's and prostitots back to the decline of raves at the turn of the century and the shift into nightclubs. Prostitots, like bro's, post images of their "EDC-ready bodies" on online EDM groups (see figures 3.9 and 3.10), accompanied with text such as the following: "Current shredding photo, what you brahs [bro's] think."

Older fans often tried to get newer fans to understand why they were against men attending EDM fests without shirts or for women going around in revealing clothes. The newer fans respond with sentiments like the following:

You're actually pretty dumb, EDC is no longer a rave but a music festival AND it happens in one of the trendiest cities in the world. Having said that, you kinda need to shut the fuck up, put on your big boy pants and attend, OR find another hole to crawl back in. Your type is the only ones who still bitch about this. Meanwhile, Pasquale has no qualms about it. Learn from the master [Pasquale Rotella]. (Male, 25, EDM Fan)

Figure 3.9   Example of Prostitots. *Source*: (Las Vegas EDC Facebook Group).

Moderators of online discussion forums also posted statements like those found in the following image (figure 3.11):

Older members responding to these posts often found themselves ostracized for "being hateful," and "not respecting others." Thus, the culture has become divided into two groups with two very different set of beliefs. While those trying to preserve the culture were often older members, many younger members were also a part of this group. Many of the resistors tried to "look out for others" but were often instead looked down upon by others. The epitome of their attitude came from newcomers who rejected the very concept of PLUR, as this quote illustrates:

Figure 3.10   Group of Bros and Prostitots. *Source*: (Las Vegas EDC Facebook Group).

> You old people need to take your PLUR and get the fuck out of here. No one wants to hear that shit. That was then and this is now. These parties are bout raging and getting fucked up. Take your hippy shit and shove it. (Male, 21, EDM Fan)

Older fans who detested overt displays of masculinity were viewed as "being judgmental," "too uptight," or accused of not "cutting loose."

It is a sad irony, given EDM's roots in largely Black and Latinx gay nightclubs, that racist and homophobic comments also are becoming increasingly prominent among EDM fans, at least online—through a process that might be termed "subcultural appropriation." One example of this process of appropriation and racism may be found in some participants' uncritical reflections on the styles they use to craft their outfits at EDM events. It is common at many EDM festivals for women and men to dress up in Native American headdresses and neon war paint (see figure 3.12). This issue sparked significant controversy among members of online message boards and Facebook groups. The overwhelming majority of members who commented on this issue, however, felt that it was not an example of racism. Responses ranged from explicitly racist comments to those who were unable to understand why some individuals might be offended:

> Quit being so butt hurt about a stupid costume. You don't see firefighters and cops complaining about people dressing like them on Halloween and they die every single day. Get over yourself, it's a costume. (Male, age unknown, EDM Fan)

Similarly, a female EDM fan had the following to say:

February 9 · Edited ·

If you can't handle good looking people showing a bit of skin, then Vegas IS NOT for you. I REPEAT, IT IS NOT FOR YOU!

Stop hating on those who feel comfortable in their own skin, regardless if they're big, small, fit, or not.

So post your sexy selfies, just don't make it XXX. lol

Like   Comment

228 people like this.

Figure 3.11   Online Moderator Defending EDC Body Ready Photos. *Source*: (Las Vegas EDC Facebook Group).

So I'm just kind of curious and want to see how other people feel because I've seen tons of controversy regarding wearing native headdresses to festivals but what about another kind of feathered headdress like this one [pictured next to

Figure 3.12   Ultra Music Festival Fan in Headress. *Source*: (Las Vegas News Bureau).

her words is a feathered headdress with a unicorn horn]? Would people find it offensive? Silly question maybe but some people can be ignorant and I person-ally don't think it bears much resemblance to a traditional headdress. It has a unicorn horn after all. (Female, age unknown, Fan)

This quotes above illustrates Bonilla-Silva's (2003) concept of color-blind racism, or how racist ideologies are rationalized by those engaging in them. These discussions most often seemed to resolve themselves with a majority of comments claiming that the displays are, "no big deal." Perhaps even more controversial is the increasing prominence of homophobic comments (see figures 3.12 and 3.13).

Those who respond negatively to such comments, or who try to advocate for tolerance, are largely chastised while individuals who make posts such as those listed above were not sanctioned, and sometimes even complimented for their looks. In the process, they end up creating a cultural system that reinforces the very things that EDM enthusiasts sought to escape. In this

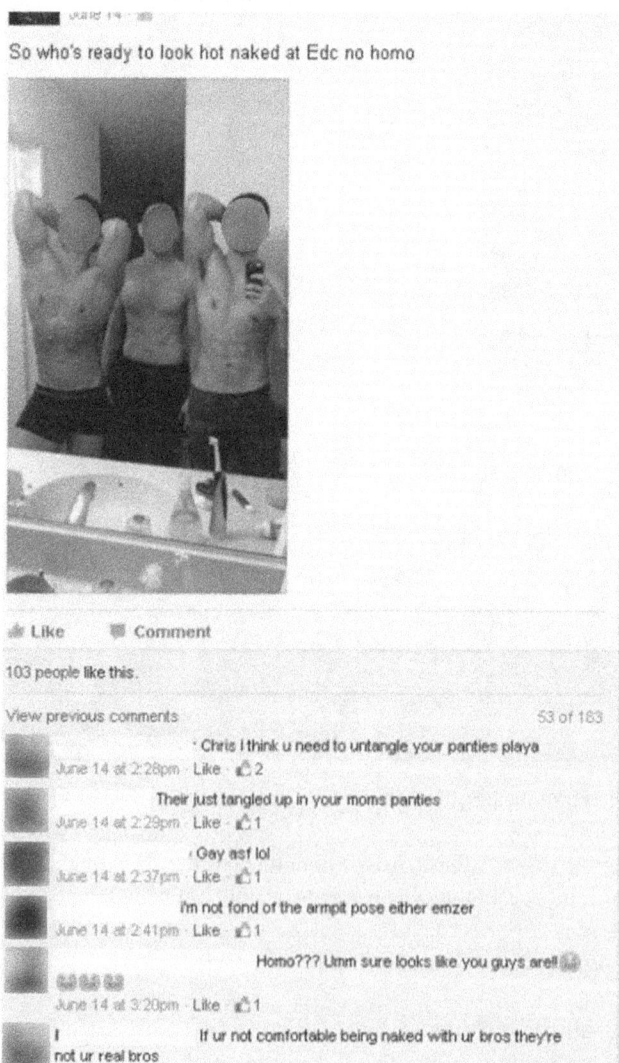

Figure 3.13   Homophobic Facebook Post. *Source*: (Las Vegas EDC Facebook Group).

sense, the EDM subculture seems to have come full circle. What was once a group formed based on principles of PLUR has been transformed into one dominated by intolerance, misogyny, and even hate speech.

CONCLUSION

This third phase in this history of the EDM subculture can best be summarized as one of increasing commodification. While the second phase saw the introduction of business interests into the subculture, in the third phase, these became the driving force. As one blogger explained:

> In short, EDM has been given a Hollywood makeover, of sorts, with brown roots frosted over, hairs plucked out, and form shaped to perfect starlet proportions. The so-called "improved" image, in turn, paints an artificial picture of the genre, with its classic traits obscured or removed. (Test 2012)

The quote captures a core feature of what Horkheimer and Adorno (1972 [1944]) saw as a major consequence of the culture industry: the colonization of authentic, indigenous cultures by corporate industries, undermining or negating their original values and critical capacity.

EDM artists came to be featured alongside established pop musicians, such as Kanye West to Madonna. This in turn not only lent EDM artists some much-needed credibility but also realigned the way they produced music to meet the demands from major music industry executives. However, some DJs criticized what they felt was the increasingly formulaic composition of EDM music. Others saw their success and increasing fortunes as a sign that they were not just talented, but justified in reaping the rewards. This is not unlike the process described by Max Weber (1930 [1905]) in *The Protestant Ethic and The Spirit of Capitalism,* in which he notes that the ideological tenants of the prosperity doctrine were necessary to usher in a more advanced form of capitalism. In a similar way, those involved with the production of the EDM subculture had a vested interest in making it more attractive to outsiders. However, with the proponents of PLUR diminished, the EDM subculture became increasingly organized as a culture industry.

Horkheimer and Adorno (1972 [1944]), like their colleague, Marcuse (1968 [1937]), also noted that art was losing its capacity to criticize the society in which it existed. In this sense, the kind of art/music produced by the culture industry inherently supports the status quo. In this phase of the EDM subculture, the commodifying features that first appeared in the second phase became a dominant characteristic, fundamentally transforming the nature of EDM and its participants. Their label as a deviant counterculture

► **EDC Las Vegas (Unofficial)**

5 hrs ·

Hey guys good news actually just bought my edc tickets with the extra money my parents gave me since they stopped giving my younger sister money since they found out that she is a lesbian.. Thanks sis see you guys under the electric sky

👍 Like   💬 Comment

84 people like this.

Lol that's funny,
Like · Reply · 5 hrs

Haha, good for you man. Fuck lesbians! *trollface*
Like · Reply · 👍 6 · 4 hrs

She's the home girl now 🤍
Like · Reply · 👍 3 · 4 hrs

Thats messed up ahha
Like · Reply · 👍 4 · 4 hrs

Hey she's getting all the pussy
Like · Reply · 👍 31 · 4 hrs

↳ 2 Replies · 4 hrs

Ehh pretty reasonable, see you next year'
Like · Reply · 4 hrs

Figure 3.14   Anti-Lesbian Attitudes. *Source*: (Las Vegas EDC Facebook Group).

was replaced by a widespread acceptance that undermined the core principles of the group. Indeed, fans trying to preserve those principles, and the movement's capacity to be critical of society, have themselves been marginalized and viewed as outdated relics of a bygone age. Instead, "bro culture" and "prostitots" became the images promoted by members themselves.

Also, industry professionals found themselves enmeshed and aligned with public officials who had once criminalized them. As part of the system of control, these individuals dismantled the politically threatening aspects of the subculture and popularized its more spectacular features (Bouchal 2012; Chasin 2000). Staging, lighting, and other aesthetic elements were refined, aiding in this process of attracting a widespread audience, and the music itself was produced in a format more digestible by mainstream audiences. In doing so, the meaningful aspects of EDM were lost from their critical impulses and turned into superficial aesthetic tropes. The true tragedy of this subculture is that those who created the culture, Black and Latinx Gay men, were marginalized as outsiders came to dominate the cultural spaces of EDM.

NOTES

1. While his biggest critic at the event was Pasqualle Rotella, his own business partner since 2006, he himself would later sell his company to Live Nation. In a twist of irony, Rotella has increasingly become a diminishing figure in his own business, while Estopinol has managed to maintain full control.

2. This is not unlike Adorno's critique of Jazz which is considered an elitist critique. However, what Adorno was criticizing, like us, was the genre was not as spontaneous as some might claim. Music genres require artists to conform to rigid styles that limits creativity.

Conclusion

We have documented the process by which the electronic dance music (EDM) subculture was transformed from a dissident music-based subculture created by queer men of color living in Chicago and Detroit to a multibillion-dollar cultural industry. Our interest in this topic stems from the more general sociological concern with how some subcultures, especially those that initially emerge as politically dissident subgroups, are transformed by outside forces that shape their organization away from their original core values. Other researchers have explored this process for the 1960s counterculture (Frank 1997), punk rock (Hebdige 1979), and even computer hackers (Steinmetz 2016). Additionally, there has been an upsurge in research on EDM which has employed a similar theoretical framework (Anderson 2009a; St John 2009; Motl 2018; Hidalgo 2022). Most important to us is how the rise of corporately produced EDM has brought about the reappearance of class, racial, gendered, and sexual hierarchies that those involved in the subculture's early formative years were purposely trying to resist (Thomas 1995).

Our findings here need not be limited just to music subcultures, but rather, we hope, might prove insightful for other similar groups and social movements. We chose to study this process within the EDM subculture because of the first authors, longtime involvement in the subculture, and because both in 2010 the largest North American dance music festival, the Electric Daisy Carnival, moved from Los Angeles to Las Vegas—where both authors were living. Also, in 2013 journalists and public relations representative for the city began calling Las Vegas the EDM capital of the world. This was spurred in large part by the growing infrastructure built to accommodate EDM productions. Increasingly resort casinos began building multimillion-dollar venues and hosting world-renowned DJs on a weekly basis. The most expensive of these, at that time, was Hakkasan Nightclub, built inside the MGM Grand Casino for $100 million

(Komenda 2013). This explosive growth provided us with a steady stream of DJs, promoters, and culture industry professionals to interview.

We chose to organize our findings into three overlapping phases. In the first phase, starting in the late 1980s until 1995, we describe the emergence of the EDM subculture in largely Black and Latinx gay nightclubs. During this period a variety of different threads came together to form the subculture including, individuals such as Frazier Clark (discussed in chapter 2), who saw EDM as a continuation of the 1960s counterculture, others who drew upon concepts from postmodern philosophy and science fiction, and still others who were experimenting with innovations in technology that opened the music production process to those previously unable to participate. Many of the artists in this period talked about how they were seeking to create a space in which they felt accepted, could express their voices, and were attempting to provide a cultural critique of society.

As these different threads converged, the value system of the EDM subculture became established as PLUM (peace, love, unity, movement) and then, later, as PLUR (peace, love, unity, respect). Some early pioneers of the movement emphasized a direct connection to the countercultural values of the music. On July 4, 1990, Adam X, born Adam Mitchell, painted the words PLUM (Peace, Love, Unity Movement) on a train car in the Bronx (Wender 2015). DJ Frankie Bones, born Frank Mitchell, retells the story of how this slogan became redefined:

> Now back to that so-called famous speech I made in The Bronx in 1993 . . . . A fight breaks out between a guy and a girl and they bump right into the table all the DJ gear was on. It was on a 1960s IBM office table, so it didn't budge, but because of the memory of Happyland [a nightclub fire in the Bronx], I completely snapped. I jumped up on the table and got on the mic and addressed the situation. We never had something like this happen in three years. I knew everyone would understand me when I said. "I'll break your f*cking faces." It was to imply I was serious. Everyone at that party knew me, so it wasn't as if I was threatening anyone with violence. The party went on into the early morning hours without incident. . . . The movement part of PLUM turned into PLUR that night by Hyperreal [an online rave chat room] 'cause the Movement was established, making the "M" become an "R" for respect. Otherwise it's one and the same. It's the only thing that connects EDM and the original scene for its duration. (Bones 2012)

Instead of more traditional protest actions, such as launching sit-ins, EDM participants carved out symbolic spaces of resistance where they could enact their vision of a society not biased due to race, class, gender, or sexual orientation. So, while on the surface the movement seemed apolitical, it in fact had a strong underlying political intent.

In these early years members' commitment to the notion of PLUR was manifested by their creating spaces with the aim of celebrating difference based on class, race, gender, and sexual orientation. DJs in this era created music embedded with philosophical notions found in emancipatory politics and postmodern science fiction. The themes within their music levied criticisms of American society, especially regarding racism and homophobia, and what they saw as a general societal intolerance of diversity. The progenitors of the subculture also had a personal connection to these criticisms, as they were part of marginalized groups due to their race, gender, and sexual orientation. In this way, the early EDM movement did resemble the 1960s counterculture who were mobilized against a variety of similar issues. While many researchers have focused on the hedonistic aspects of the subculture, there was also this deeper purpose within the subculture.

Early EDM enthusiasts could thus justify calling themselves a counterculture, as they consciously acted against the dominant culture. Sociologically, the EDM subculture might also be described as a social movement due to its members' commitment to active resistance and attempt to create broader social change. While to outsider observers they were merely organizing hedonistic celebrations, to the participants themselves they were creating a safe space for those who felt judged on the basis of class, race, gender, or sexual orientation could find refuge. The EDM subculture stressed the rejection of celebrity culture, encouraged new forms of community, and codified these practices as PLUR.

There were, however counternarratives that we found that obscured the political implications of EDM. Instead of seeing the formation of something akin to a counterculture, they chose to emphasize the hedonism that EDM embodied. As one blog post illustrates:

> Other generations have all the luck. Their subcultural miscreants were usually tied to some sort of ideological principles. You know, peace, free love, that sort of thing. It's almost as if the preceding counter-cultural movements took all the good visionary underpinnings and we were stuck sorting through the remnants bin. Our take on rebellious youth culture amounted to Seattle Grunge culture and Euro-techno ravers. We may not have been as idealistic as the hippies who came before us, but it could have been worse. After all, we could have been pseudo-intellectual fake glasses-sporting ironic t-shirt clad hipsters. There were some vague alliances between rave culture and principles, but the connection was fuzzy at best. At its heart, rave culture represented the happy-go-lucky invincibility that characterized the 90s. You know you're getting older when you start drawing broad metaphors between youth culture and the state of the economy, but it's an aging leap I'm willing to make. Raving was youth culture in its purest, least dilute form: wild, irresponsible, and generally under contempt of adults everywhere. (Children of the 90s 2010)

We also interviewed DJs and promoters who also repeated this narrative. However, when pressed further on the issue, they often responded by saying that early EDM was political in so much as how law enforcement responded to them. They were, in effect, articulating the points made decades earlier by Howard Becker and his colleagues in what has become known as the labeling theory perspective (Tannenbarum 1938; Becker 1973; Kitsuse 1975; Plummer 2011). We also think that, individuals we interviewed on this point may have been trying to reduce the cognitive dissonance brought on from criticisms of "selling out." While some who used this narrative have suggested that arguments concerning EDM political significance are misplaced, this was rejected by most of our research subjects. Moreover, we found many instances of active political resistance on the part those we interviewed. When considered in its entirety, there can be no doubt that EDM was formed, at least in part, as a reaction to larger structural issues that impacted members of the group. It was only with the commodification of the subculture that EDM began to become less politically oriented.

Subcultures and countercultures always emerge in reaction to larger historical and structural contexts (Hebdige 1979). The blog post above hints at the fact that early EDM's optimism, enshrined in the values of PLUR and the incorporation of a style that emphasized childhood youth through bright colors, were the product of a robust economy. However, recall that early EDM enthusiasts were disproportionally queer men of color. Thus, despite a positive economy, the progenitors of the culture will still experiencing both overt and structural forms of discrimination as well as the impacts of other social issues. These included the AIDS crisis of the 1980s, the end of the Cold War, the first Gulf War, the LA Riots, and a series of natural disasters such as Hurricane Andrew in 1992, massive flooding of the Mississippi River in 1993, and a 1993 eastern seaboard blizzard. Sociologically, subcultures give those impacted by unstable societal conditions, such as these a way in which to insulate themselves. The 1960s counterculture was a response to the Vietnam War and political injustices, the 1980s punk movement was a way of responding to harsh economic conditions, and the EDM subculture offered a way for subculturalists to resist racism and homophobia and a neoliberal economic system that was extremely adept at atomizing human relations (Conner and MacMurray 2022).

EDM also emerged in the shadow of an era that was politically conservative. The two most powerful leaders of the two most powerful countries, UK prime minister Margret Thatcher and US president Ronald Reagan, introduced a number of public policies that would have disastrous ramifications for years to come. These included the war on drugs (fought in both the United Kingdom and United States), deregulation, the cutting of public funding, a rising national deficit, and an aggressive foreign policy. In the wake of these larger historical forces, the early members I talked to described general feelings of rejection and isolation—what sociologists call "anomie" (Durkheim 1951 [1897]). For its supporters, the EDM subculture gave them a place where they could develop a positive sense of self, or in their own words, "a place where 'freaks can be freaks'" (Female, 45, DJ). As one self-described historian of the scene recalled:

> If you were different in that time [1990–1995], you didn't really have a place you could go. The reason the culture took off was because we gave others a home. We didn't have legitimate venues, and most club owners saw us as weirdos, so we had to create our own spaces. (Male, 39, Fan)

By establishing the EDM subculture, members rejected the values of their parent culture, expressed a collective longing for relief from the social strains mentioned above, and sometimes even demonstrated active resistance by collectively organizing. Some music critics (Brewster and Broughton 1999; Reynolds 1999) have similarly pointed out the countercultural underpinnings of the EDM subculture as being grounded in the twin musical influences of the sensual (house), and the critical (techno). To them, early EDM culture was about finding an escape through pleasure, combined with a social commentary on the current state of society in both the United States and the United Kingdom.

While larger structural conditions often help shape artistic and other cultural movements, their uniqueness comes from how subgroups in society respond to those changes. Punk, for example, reappropriated and redefined cultural objects to create something that would be an important innovation in music and in political thought for decades after it was declared dead. The same too can be said of EDM, though the difference lay in their use of playfulness, bright colors, and optimism. Unlike Punks and Goths, who leaned into notions of death and decay as metaphors for the society that was crumbling around them (Hodkinson 2002), EDM chose a slightly alternative pathway. In a society that was increasingly promoting a singular definition of success, EDM presented enthusiasts with an alternative vision built on the remains of the 1960s countercultural ideas of "free love." They also stood against unbridled capitalism, which they saw as the source for many of society's problems.

EDM participants carved out symbolic spaces of resistance where they could enact their vision of a society not biased due to class, race, gender, or sexual orientation (Kosmicki 2001). The impact of this was the creation of a subculture that celebrated differences and provided a space where individuals from different disparate backgrounds could come together. Matos (2015) cites a recent interview he conducted with Neil Ollivierra, a Detroit techno musician:

Mojo made it okay for young black people to listen to "white" music . . . . When they saw that was possible, they realized you could tear down similar boundaries in terms of fashion and music and literature and style and friendships and culture. They realized you could change all kinds of stuff about your life. (cited in Matos 2015: 8)

By being critical of capitalism, EDM participants also reduced the barriers to join in the subculture. Venues that were "acquired" for free sound systems that were donated, and music that they re-appropriated or created themselves meant that they owned the subculture. This critical attitude may have been a by-product of a decline in the middle-class and blue-collar manufacturing work leaving Chicago and Detroit.[1] This also meant that there were a large amount of abandoned factories which EDM organizers could utilize, illegally, to hold their events.

A third influence that was instrumental in the rise to the EDM subculture was a cultural zeitgeist that was fueled by an optimism for technology. New computer technologies were making musical equipment much more affordable and also provided new innovations in other musical technology that EDM DJs used to create music—especially the splicing together of previously recorded music. Like the abandoned factories they used to organize their events, old pop songs and hits of an earlier generation could be repurposed and combined with new elements. In this way, EDM DJs exemplified postmodern notions of pastiche and montage, using the discarded elements of pop culture in such a way as to create something entirely new (Denzin 1994). This is perhaps what drove so many individuals involved with EDM to see themselves not as simply cultural innovators, but the vanguard of a full-on revolution made possible by new technologies. While it would take the better part of a decade before public widespread adoption of the internet would occur, even in these formative years the concept of greater connectivity was being foreshadowed. Indeed, much of today's internet culture was established during this time period, and EDM was highly influential in that development (Beran 2019)[2].

In the second phase, from approximately 1995 to 2003, the location of EDM events shifted from clandestine venues such as abandoned warehouses to spaces deemed more "legitimate," with licensing fees, ticket sales, liability insurance, and other legal requirements. The shift was triggered largely by media coverage that focused on sensationalized stories of widespread drug use, to which politicians and law enforcement responded by passing and enforcing legislation that forced EDM organizers into more legitimate venues. Moving into more conventional venues, in turn, attracted larger audiences and profits, which attracted the attention of the music industry, anxious to get in on the new money-making opportunities. The introduction of the RAVE Act, by then-senator Joe Biden, sought to criminalize the activities of the subculture. This act, however, also inadvertently led to EDM's "salvation" as a more conventionally organized entity. Thus, organizers in this era faced a difficult decision: they could go legitimate, but this would fundamentally alter the nature of EDM events. Many who went along with these changes did so thinking they would be able to preserve the autonomy of EDM and its core ideas of PLUR while also shielding the movement from encroaching law enforcement agencies.

Moving into legitimate spaces, however, created something of a schism among members of the subculture, who felt it was compromising its core values and beliefs. This move also brought with it the unwanted presence of outsiders. As Anderson (2009a) found, this made women feel more like sexual objects, something they were trying to avoid by participating in EDM, and increasingly marginalized queer people of color who were responsible for founding the subculture (see also Mears 2021). Moreover, these newcomers were largely unaware of the subculture, and as their numbers increased the organizers began to increasingly cater to this new demographic. Because EDM promoters and organizers had to use licensed venues and pay for security and other services, they began having to focus on maximizing ticket sales whereas before their events were free or charged only a nominal fee.

As the corporate music industry became drawn to EDM, its professionals also began to devise ways in which the music could be made more marketable to outsiders. Many DJs embraced the involvement of big companies, who provided them access to state-of-the-art equipment. However, such access also brought with it added pressures to produce a more profitable product. Thus, according to many members, the music in this era began to sound more polished and commercial, undermining original notions of aesthetic authenticity. The large music corporations also changed how DJs performed, by restructuring EDM events to look more like rock concerts. This was an important way in which EDM was made attractive to American audiences. As this format was only slightly different from what conventional music fans were used to seeing. Errol Kolosine, an EDM industry label professional, explained the importance of this:

> The Brothers' live show offered salvation. Black people, white people, gay people, straight people, frat boys—you name it. Everybody here is equal, and the music is what is bringing everybody in here together. It occurred to me, if I get enough people to experience this, we can't lose. (cited in Matos 2015: 213)

Here we are providing a glimpse into how the cultural appropriation of EDM, created by queer men of color, was reforged and made attractive to white audiences. While in the earlier era EDM culture emphasized bringing together disparate groups together, in this phase it became more focused on monetizing the music. More importantly, this example underscores the tension that existed in this period between authenticity, race and sexual identity, and commodification.

EDM became more professionalized, with formal contracts, slick advertising, and elaborate stage designs. DJs also began to rely on advertising professionals to market their images and appeal as likeable celebrities. While, in the previous era, DJs were largely anonymous figures, their image and attractiveness now became a central focus. A significant result of this change concerned the demographic makeup of DJs, from being mostly Gay Black and Latinx men, to being mostly white males from European countries (especially Germany, the Netherlands, Poland, and Sweden).

A few promoters had already begun to consider the use of more legitimate venues, even before the introduction of the RAVE act. As one we talked with articulated:

> Everybody realized that we had to get legitimate, because basically we had 600 people with no security, no liquor license. At some point, any human being is going to be like, "oh shit, this is dangerous. I'm going to get fucking sued, right?" There is a tipping point. (Male, 40, Promoter)

Thus, event organizers could no longer utilize clandestine, often illegal spaces (i.e., warehouses, cornfields, and desert spaces). This shift, at least initially, was mostly due not to a desire for profits, but out of concerns for safety. There were also other benefits that came out of moving to more legitimate spaces:

> I went to a party in New York City. It was either 1995 or 1996. An Electric Zoo type of event. We drove from New Orleans to go to this party. It was huge with 70,000 people. To us, the best thing ever, right? It was at a stadium and legitimized. Not a dingy warehouse. Could get shut down. In the 90's, when it really got legit, is when I moved to these bigger venues. It became an overall better experience for people involved. It's not like a warehouse, Port-o-Potties, no safety, no insurance, no liquor license. It'd grown too big and we moved into legitimate venues to help make it grow. (Male, 40, Promoter)

At the same time, however, the music was made more accessible and commercialized, leading to a shift in the demographic makeup of fans toward predominately white, middle-class, heterosexual men (Motl 2018; Little et al. 2018; Wiltsher 2016; Park 2015). These newcomers often had little or no collective commitment to the core values of the subculture. Despite these changes, some members still tried to maintain a degree of autonomy and commitment to the core values, but they were becoming a distinct minority.

Event organizers also faced a tough sell to fans accustomed to free or very inexpensive admission prices. This also problematized the actions of those trying to maintain political resistance strategies and the core values of the subculture. With this move, however, the very notion of EDM as an "underground" subculture was called into question as it was now easier to survey. It was also attracting more attention from other public officials. Thus, sociologically speaking, what the RAVE Act, and other actions on the part of public officials, did for the EDM subculture was to put into place a set of rules that impacted the organization of the subculture. This second phase was also significant because it brought significant cultural changes that would impact its future development. The use of legitimate spaces took EDM out of a sharing economy and placed it into the larger political economy of nightclubs and the entertainment industry. Orienting EDM enthusiasts to the logics of commodification and consumption would lay the foundations necessary to propel the subculture into a full-blown culture industry in the third phase.

In the third phase, extending from 2004 up to the present, EDM has become fully corporatized. This phase of the development of the subculture is best characterized as a full-blown culture industry in the sense first described by Horkheimer and Adorno ([1944] 1972). They described the culture industry in terms of the increasing tendency for culture to be commodified and organized using standardizing practices, which are masked by superficial differentiating characteristics they refer to as pseudo-individualization. This phase was made possible by the creation of an infrastructure that would allow EDM to be produced on a scale that made it profitable and by marketing EDM's attractive features to mass audiences.

Once promoters began reimagining themselves as business owners, rather than just as participants in the movement, other aspects of the subculture also were more easily commodified. In this sense promoters were comparable to third-world compradors (Wallerstein 2004), promising EDM enthusiasts that these changes would benefit rather than harm them, all the while profiting from a system that they helped design. While some maintain that they had no other choice and that they couldn't have possibly known the impact of their decisions, the end result has been an erosion of the values of the subculture in favor of consumerism and profitability. Moreover, most EDM promoters that we spoke with were fine hosting EDM events in nightclubs in which they could maintain control of the subculture. However, promoters face continued pressure by nightclub owners who were increasingly trying to exert control over them—often in the form of asking for a greater percentage of admission receipts, a guaranteed amount of alcohol sales, or through facility fees.

Thus, this third phase was in many ways set in motion by promoters who sought to maintain autonomy. While the promoters and artists we spoke with often defined "autonomy" in terms of artistic creativity, some noted that this also allowed them greater control of profits. Instead, nightclubs promoters began using state-managed facilities such as arenas, fairgrounds, amphitheaters, and larger outdoor venues. This provided them with greater flexibility, creativity, and control over their events. At the same time, however, rising costs have forced promoters to seek corporate sponsors, which meant relinquishing much of their control to these benefactors.

At the same time, DJs were increasingly trying to make their performances more professional. In this instance, "professional" meant making their performances multisensory experiences, which have become increasingly extravagant thanks to technological innovations. These include the use of laser lights, LED screens, drones that could be programed and utilized in lighting, 3D holograms, interactive performers, fireworks, and multimillion-dollar stage designs. The critical French philosopher Guy Debord (1967) theorized that these kinds of sensory experiences were part of a contemporary phenomenon he called "the spectacle." According to Debord, the spectacle was taking primacy over genuine human experiences. Like the members of the Frankfurt School, Debord felt that this kind of cultural phenomenon was robbing art of its critical capacity and undermining the kinds of contemporary emancipatory politics needed for social change. Some of these concerns were also becoming the subject of internal debates within the EDM subculture.

One of the major concerns expressed by those we interviewed (fans, promoters, and DJs) was the decline in artistic creativity. Even some major promoters of the genre have noted that, at EDM music festivals, many DJs often play many of the same compositions. As some of those we interviewed discussed with us, instead of exposing audiences to new music, DJs were increasingly playing the music they felt the crowd wanted to hear, resulting in a kind of homogenization and repetition among musical performers. This shift, however, has made the role of DJs highly profitable, at least for the more successful ones.

Since the early 2000s there has been a great deal of discussion among EDM enthusiasts about how to better incorporate visually stimulating elements into events. Some DJs have placed the burden of these spectacular productions on promoters or club venues. This has resulted in higher ticket prices as these new visual elements are introduced. At the same time, increasingly sophisticated technologies have emerged by manufacturers catering to DJs. As a result, many aspects of their performances have become at least partially automated. Live performers can now flawlessly and automatically transition between different songs and producers have access to a wide range of tools making EDM production far more effortless. Some EDM DJs themselves have pointed out a certain irony here, since they now make more money than ever but they do far less work as they only have to push "play."

While in the first era DJs often had to manufacture tools for their performances—splicing together tape, manipulating turntables designed for non-commercial purposes, and in other ways—today they have access to sophisticated technologies which allow them to move seamlessly between different musical compositions. Many computer programs can analyze, select, and do much of the work that DJs developed over the years. We heard many DJs argue that "anyone can be a DJ these days." The impact of this, however has been the increasing presence of outsiders, who have become attracted by the promise of fame and fortune.[3]

Politically, the successes experienced by EDM producers have been met with open arms by public officials who once criminalized the subculture. Mayors, police chiefs, and other public officials now play an active role in the planning and promotion of EDM events like the Electric Daisy Carnival held annually in Las Vegas. Promoters gained this acceptance by making the argument that they could provide struggling urban economies with significant revenue from EDM tourism. The tradeoff, however, has been a further reduction of the original core values that placed political and social change at the forefront of the subculture. A good example of this is how many fans today openly embrace the presence of local law-enforcement agents by engaging them in subcultural practices, such as the exchange of kandi bracelets. Thus, the EDM subculture has now been brought into line with many of the societal standards its enthusiasts originally resisted.

While not all fans have embraced these changes in the character of EDM events, an overwhelming majority now seem to accept them without question. This has led not only to the erosion of original notions of PLUR, but often to their replacement by racist, sexist, homophobic, and other biased views of newcomers. These newer members are also often openly hostile toward older fans who have tried to preserve and protect the original values of the subculture. In light of this, many longtime enthusiasts have stopped attending EDM events.

SOCIOLOGICAL SIGNIFICANCE

Other studies of music-based subcultures focus, almost exclusively, on the role of increasing popularity in diminishing countercultural values (Bennett 1999; Epstein 2004; Anderson 2009). In this research, however, at least in the case of EDM, we discovered a more complicated process in which structural factors such as the mass media, public officials (politicians and law enforcement), and the corporate music industry played a major role in this transformation. Negative, sensationalized media coverage provoked a repressive response by politicians and law enforcement. This, in turn, forced

EDM event organizers into more legitimate venues, bringing EDM to the attention of major music corporations. This, in turn, transformed the way the music was produced, promoted, and consumed, while bringing in a mass audience mostly unaware or uninterested in the sub/countercultural values of the original EDM enthusiasts. Somewhat ironically, however, while these values, represented by the PLUR slogan, have largely disappeared, illegal drug use, which provoked the moral panic originally promoted by the media, has become more significant.

Another major contribution of this study is our focus on the vital role played by industry professionals. Early event organizers, promoters, and DJs saw themselves as an integral part of the EDM subculture with little distance between themselves and fans. However, these individuals both transformed and were transformed by progressive integration into the culture industry. While some of them struggled to remain true to the group's core values, others fully embraced their role in the new corporate model. Similarly, some fans resisted the commodifying tendencies of the culture industry by trying to educate newer EDM enthusiasts. Many of these individuals, however, were not only unaware of the history of the music, but were openly hostile toward those trying to preserve the core values of the original subculture.

We also sought to more thoroughly understand the impact of mass media. The media, in fact, played an important catalytic role in each phase, shaping the public's views, as well as the reaction by public officials, toward the EDM subculture. In the first phase, the media portrayed EDM followers as a deviant subculture characterized by rampant drug use and a general rejection of societal norms. In the second phase, continued negative media coverage, both locally and nationally, began to depict law enforcement as inept. While this had an unintended effect of making the music more popular, it also resulted in repressive legislation and enforcement that criminalized many of the activities of the subculture. The culmination of public officials' reactions in the creation of the RAVE Act. Today, the media promotes a respectable image of EDM, exclusively as a profitable segment of the culture industry, with little to no mention of its countercultural roots. This is illustrated by images of local law enforcement and politicians embracing, figuratively and literally, EDM industry professionals and fans.

Theoretically, we have tried to provide a more nuanced discussion of how the culture industry works. In their original account, Horkheimer and Adorno pointed out the limits of the analogy between culture and industry but they offered little by way of discussion. As our study shows, at each phase of development, the EDM subculture moved further and further away from its core values of PLUR. This process was the result of a complicated interplay of factors, both within the structure of the subculture and in other larger changes. Rather than understand this as a unilateral process, we have attempted to show that off ramps existed in which the fate of EDM might have developed differently. However, the external forces shaping the development of EDM eventually overcame this resistance, allowing it to develop into a culture industry.

In a later essay written by Adorno (1967 [1975]), he argued that the culture industry never completely commodifies the areas it colonizes, but rather contains some form of semblance to its former self. The full commodification of cultural spaces, he argues, would result in resistance on the part of the audience. We also found evidence of this as some, especially older, EDM enthusiasts try to maintain some spirit of resistance, but within the broader context of EDM this seems to be increasingly marginalized. This include holding smaller parties and events, but just as in the early days when police harassed participants, many of these events are often shut down—using some of the same tactics the police have always used (Kosmicki 2001; Petiau and Garcia 2015). Thus, rather than rebuting the culture industry thesis, this evidence continued, through limited resistance reinforces our use of it to interpret our findings.

A variety of subgroups have, to varying degrees, relied on market-based strategies to reduce the moral stigma placed on them by more powerful members of society. These include the LGBTQ movement, computer hackers, and other music subcultures. Like the EDM subculture, each of these groups have faced internal divisions as to whether or not market-based strategies have resulted in a loss of their core values (Fox 1987). It is no wonder, then, that EDM organizers, such as those who organize the Electric Daisy Carnival in Las Vegas, or Disco Donnie Estopinal, mentioned in chapter 3, present themselves not as business persons but just "one of the fans." Moreover, their claims to be creating an authentic EDM experience are integrated into their marketing strategy vis a vis commodified resistance. This is what Marcuse (1964) described as repressive desublimation, in which the elements of social critique are removed from commodified spectacles like contemporary music festivals.

We also sought to understand how marginalized groups within subcultures are transformed over time. Clearly, the price for greater recognition and legitimacy, at least in the case of EDM, has come at the expense of their fight for a more egalitarian, if not utopian version of the world. This, in turn, leads to the broader question of why some subcultures seem to reproduce the same systems of inequality that persist within the dominant culture. In the early days of EDM hierarchies of status were relatively flat, but over time class position became a key component in who participated in the culture. As the movement became more commodified, it also introduced some of the misogynistic, homophobic, and racist tendencies found elsewhere in society. In this way, this study speaks to the corrosive impact that the commodification of culture can have on marginalized groups as they become more widely accepted, even as many members of the EDM subculture attempted to counteract the influence of these outside commodifying forces jeopardizing their core values. Resistance, it would seem, is an ongoing struggle that must continuously be renewed as movements mature, and a major trade-off exists between political resistance and acceptance by the broader society.

Despite conducting this research over several years, there were several limits that future research should seek to overcome. Feminist critiques of the study of music subcultures note that men often face a privileged voice in this kind of research (Motl 2018; Hidalgo 2022; Mears 2021). While we have attempted to recruit and champion the voice of women in this study, most of our sources were men. In discussing this with our research subjects after fieldwork had concluded, they noted that the way EDM has been historically structured has meant women have tended to be marginalized in the movement—even in its formative years. Secondly, our reliance on qualitative data, including participants' recollections of the early EDM movement, might have been improved with more quantitative data. These especially include questions as to just how much the EDM subculture has changed over time. However, since data from those early formative years is impossible to obtain, these questions may never be answered more deeply beyond what we have tried to do here. Additionally, even contemporary reports on data on events such as EDC rely heavily upon whether the company that produces it will collect and release that information. However, those participants who reviewed drafts of this monograph, the resounding answer we got back was, "You got it right, that's it! That's the story of how it all went down."

NOTES

1. This may also help explain differences in the sounds produced in Chicago and Detroit. The two cities were impacted differently by deindustrialization. Chicago, which was far less impacted than Detroit, became the home for House, which was far more focused on a kind of spiritual-sexual release, and was more melodic. Detroit, by contrast, developed techno which was not only harsher sounding but was infused with elements of science fiction that stressed the importance of resistance.

2. Some have even traced these developments as laying the foundations for widespread conspiracism and right-wing movements like QAnon (Beran 2019).

3. This includes celebrities, social media influencers, actors, NBA stars, and many others with no attachment to the subculture.

Appendix

The Rave Act

	Calendar No. 453
107TH CONGRESS 2D SESSION	**S. 2633**

To prohibit an individual from knowingly opening, maintaining, managing, controlling, renting, leasing, making available for use, or profiting from any place for the purpose of manufacturing, distributing, or using any controlled substance, and for other purposes.

IN THE SENATE OF THE UNITED STATES

JUNE 18, 2002

Mr. BIDEN (for himself, Mr. GRASSLEY, Mr. HATCH, Mr. LEAHY, and Mr. DURBIN) introduced the following bill; which was read twice and referred to the Committee on the Judiciary

JUNE 27, 2002

Reported by Mr. LEAHY, without amendment

A BILL

To prohibit an individual from knowingly opening, maintaining, managing, controlling, renting, leasing, making available for use, or profiting from any place for the purpose of manufacturing, distributing, or using any controlled substance, and for other purposes.

Be it ENACTED *by the* SENATE AND *House of* REPRESENTAtives *of the* UNITED *States of America* IN CONGRESS *assembled,*

SEC. 1. SHORT TITLE

This Act may be cited as the "Reducing Americans' Vulnerability to Ecstasy Act of 2002' or the "RAVE Act'.'

SEC. 2. FINDINGS.

Congress finds the following:

(1) Each year tens of thousands of young people are initiated into the drug culture at "rave" parties or events (all-night, alcohol-free dance parties typically featuring loud, pounding dance music).

(2) Some raves are held in dance clubs with only a handful of people in attendance. Other raves are held at temporary venues such as warehouses, open fields, or empty buildings, with tens of thousands of people present.

(3) The trafficking and use of "club drugs," including 3, 4-Methylenedioxymethamphetamine (Ecstasy or MDMA), Ketamine hydrochloride (Ketamine), Flunitrazepam (Rohypnol), and Gamma hydroxybutyrate (GHB), is deeply embedded in the rave culture.

(4) Many rave promoters go to great lengths to try to portray their events as alcohol-free parties that are safe places for young adults to go to dance with friends, and some even go so far as to hire off-duty, uniformed police officers to patrol outside of the venue to give parents the impression that the event is safe.

(5) Despite such efforts to convince parents that raves are safe, promotional flyers with slang terms for Ecstasy or pictures of Ecstasy pills send the opposite message to teenagers, and in effect promote Ecstasy along with the rave. According to the National Drug Intelligence Center, raves have become little more than a way to exploit American youth.

(6) Because rave promoters know that Ecstasy causes the body temperature in a user to rise and as a result causes the user to become very thirsty, many rave promoters facilitate and profit from flagrant drug use at rave

parties or events by selling over-priced bottles of water and charging entrance fees to "chill-rooms" where users can cool down.

(7) To enhance the effects of the drugs that patrons have ingested, rave promoters sell—

(A) neon glow sticks;

(B) massage oils;

(C) menthol nasal inhalers; and

(D) pacifiers that are used to combat the involuntary teeth clenching associated with Ecstasy.

(8) Ecstasy is the most popular of the club drugs associated with raves. Thousands of teenagers are treated for overdoses and Ecstasy-related health problems in emergency rooms each year. The Drug Abuse Warning Network reports that Ecstasy mentions in emergency visits grew 1040 percent between 1994 and 1999.

(9) Ecstasy damages neurons in the brain which contain serotonin, the chemical responsible for mood, sleeping and eating habits, thinking processes, aggressive behavior, sexual function, and sensitivity to pain. According to the National Institute on Drug Abuse, this can lead to long-term brain damage that is still evident 6 to 7 years after Ecstasy use.

(10) (An Ecstasy overdose is characterized by an increased heart rate, hypertension, renal failure, visual hallucinations, and overheating of the body (some Ecstasy deaths have occurred after the core body temperature of the user goes as high as 110 degrees, causing all major organ systems to shut down and muscles to breakdown), and may cause heart attacks, strokes, and seizures.

SEC. 3. OFFENSES

(a) IN GENERAL.—Section 416(a) of the Controlled Substances Act (21 U.S.C. 856(a)) is amended—

(1) in paragraph (1), by striking "open or maintain any place" and inserting "open, lease, rent, use, or maintain any place, whether permanently or temporarily"; and

(2) by striking paragraph (2) and inserting the following:

"(2) manage or control any place, whether permanently or temporarily, either as an owner, lessee, agent, employee, occupant, or mortgagee, and knowingly and intentionally rent, lease, profit from, or make available for use, with or without compensation, the place for the purpose of unlawfully manufacturing, storing, distributing, or using a controlled substance."

(b) TECHNICAL AMENDMENT—The heading to section 416 of the Controlled Substances Act (21 U.S.C. 856) is amended to read as follows:

"SEC. 416. MAINTAINING DRUG-INVOLVED PREMISES."

(c) CONFORMING AMENDMENT—The table of contents to title II of the Comprehensive Drug Abuse and Prevention Act of 1970 is amended by striking the item relating to section 416 and inserting the following:

"Sec. 416. Maintaining Drug-involved Premises."

SEC. 4. CIVIL PENALTY AND EQUITABLE RELIEF FOR MAINTAINING DRUG-INVOLVED PREMISES.

Section 416 of the Controlled Substances Act (21 U.S.C. 856) is amended by adding at the end the following:

"(d)(1) Any person who violates subsection (a) shall be subject to a civil penalty of not more than the greater of—

"(A) $250,000; or

"(B) Two times the gross receipts, either known or estimated, that were derived from each violation that is attributable to the person.

"(2) If a civil penalty is calculated under paragraph (1)(B), and there is more than 1 defendant, the court may apportion the penalty between multiple violators, but each violator shall be jointly and severally liable for the civil penalty under this subsection.

"(e) Any person who violates subsection (a) shall be subject to declaratory and injunctive remedies as set forth in section 403(f)."

SEC. 5. DECLARATORY AND INJUNCTIVE REMEDIES.

Section 403(f)(1) of the Controlled Substances Act (21 U.S.C. 843(f)(1)) is amended by striking "this section or section 402" and inserting "this section, section 402, 25 or 416."

SEC. 6. SENTENCING COMMISSION GUIDELINES.

The United States Sentencing Commission shall—

(1) review the Federal sentencing guidelines with respect to offenses involving gamma hydroxybutyric acid (GHB);

(2) consider amending the Federal sentencing guidelines to provide for increased penalties such that those penalties reflect the seriousness of offenses involving GHB and the need to deter them; and

(3) take any other action the Commission considers necessary to carry out this section.

SEC. 7. AUTHORIZATION OF APPROPRIATIONS FOR A DEMAND REDUCTION COORDINATOR.

There is authorized to be appropriated $5,900,000 to the Drug Enforcement Administration of the Department of Justice for the hiring of a special agent in each State to serve as a Demand Reduction Coordinator.

SEC. 8. AUTHORIZATION OF APPROPRIATIONS FOR DRUG EDUCATION.

There is authorized to be appropriated such sums as necessary to the Drug Enforcement Administration of the Department of Justice to educate youth, parents, and other interested adults about the drugs associated with raves.

Calendar No. 453

107TH CONGRESS
2D SESSION

S.2633

A BILL

To prohibit an individual from knowingly opening, maintaining, managing, controlling, renting, leasing, making available for use, or profiting from any place for the purpose of manufacturing, distributing, or using any controlled substance, and for other purposes.

JUNE 27, 2002
Reported without amendment

References

Adorno, Theodor. 1975 [1967]. "Culture Industry Reconsidered." Translated by Anson G. Rabinbach. *New German Critique* Autumn (6): 12–19.

Adorno, Theodor. 1991 [1977]. "Free Time." In *The Culture Industry: Selected Essays on Mass Culture,* edited by J.M. Bernstein, 187–196. Routledge: New York.

Ahrens, Deborah. 2013. "Drug Panics in the Twenty-First Century: Ecstasy, Prescription Drugs, and the Reframing of the War on Drugs." *Albany Government Law Review* 6 (2): 398–436.

Anderson, Tammy. 2009a. *Rave Culture: The Alteration and Decline of a Philadelphia Music Scene.* Philadelphia: Temple University Press.

Anderson, Tammy. 2009b. "Understanding the Alteration and Decline of a Music Scene: Observations from Rave Culture." *Sociological Forum* 24 (2): 307–336.

Anderson, Tammy. 2014. "Molly, Deaths, and the Failed War on Drugs." *Contexts* 13 (4): 48–53.

Anderson, Tammy and Phillip R. Kavanaugh. 2007. "A Rave Review: Conceptual Interests and Analytical Shifts in Research on Rave Culture." *Sociology Compass* 1 (2): 499–519.

Bain, Katie. 2013. "Why Are Old School Electronic Artists Annoyed With EDM?" *Village Voice,* May 14. Retrieved May 17, 2013 (http://www.laweekly.com/music/why-are-old-school-electronic-artists-annoyed-with-edm-4170361).

Beacon Economics. 2012. "Electric Daisy Carnival Las Vegas 2012 Economic Impact Analysis." Retrieved June 10, 2013 (http://www.insomniac.com/reports /2012.10.01_EDC_LV_ 2012.pdf).

Becker, Howard. 1963. *Outsiders: Studies in the Sociology of Deviance.* New York: The Free Press.

Becker, Howard. 1967. "Whose Side Are We On?" *Social Problems* 14 (3): 239–247.

Bennett, Andy. 1999. "Subcultures or Neo-Tribes? Rethinking the Relationship between Youth, Style and Musical Taste." *Sociology* 33 (3): 599–617.

Bennett, Andy and Richard A. Peterson. 2004. *Introduction.* In *Music Scenes: Local, Translocal, and Virtual,* edited by Andy Bennett and Richard A. Peterson, 1–15. Nashville, TN: Vanderbilt University Press.

Beran, Dale. 2019. *It Came From Something Awful*. New York, NY: Macmillian Press.

Bentley, Jason, Rafael Weiss, Senthil Chidambaram, Simon Rust Lamb, Swedish Egil, and Zel McCarthy. 2014. "EDM in Pop Culture: The Foundation of a Global Movement." Presented at the annual meeting of the EDMbiz Conference, Las Vegas, Nevada, July 08.

Blackman, Shane. 2007. "Youth Subcultural Theory: A Critical Engagement with the Concept, its Origins and Politics, from the Chicago School to Postmodernism." *Journal of Youth Studies* 8 (1): 1–20.

Bonilla-Silva, Eduardo. 2014. *Racism Without Racists: Color-blind Racism and the Persistence of Racial Inequality in America*. 4th edition. Lanham: Rowman & Littlefield Publishers, Inc.

Bouchal, Jakob. 2012. "EDM- the Worst Thing That has Ever Happened to Electronic Dance Music?" *Disco Demons,* September 9. Retrieved July 3, 2014 (http://www.discodemons.net/2012/09/09/edm-vs-electronic-dance-music/).

Bones, Frankie. 2012. "The History of P.L.U.R." *Peace Love Unity Revisited.* Retrieved June 16, 2015 (http://frankiebones.tumblr.com/).

Bredow, Gary. 2006. *High Tech Soul: The Creation of Techno Music*. DVD. Detroit: Plexifilm.

Brewster, Bill and Frank Broughton. 1999. *Last Night a DJ Saved My Life: The History of the Disc Jockey*. New York: Grove Press.

Bryman, Alan. 1999. "The Disneyization of Society." *The Sociological Review* 47 (1): 25–47.

Budnick, Dean and Josh Baron. 2011. *Ticket Masters: The Rise of the Concert Industry and How The Public Got Scalped*. Toronto: ECW Press.

Bulmer, Martin. 1984. *The Chicago School of Sociology: Institutionalization, Diversity, and the Rise of Sociological Research*. Chicago: University of Chicago Press.

Buckland, Fiona. 2002. *Impossible Dance: Club Culture and Queer World-Making*. Middletown: Wesleyan.

Centers for Disease Control (CDC). 2010. "Ecstasy Overdose at a New Year's Even Rave-Los Angeles, California, 2010." *Morbidity and Mortality Weekly Report* 59 (22): 677–681.

Cerni, Mary Grace. 2014. "10 Unforgettable People at Lightning in a Bottle." *LA Weekly,* May 27. Accessed September 5, 2022 (https://www.laweekly.com/10-unforgettable-people-at-lightning-in-a-bottle/).

Chasin, Alexandra. 2000. *Selling Out: The Gay & Lesbian Movement Goes to Market*. New York: St. Martin's Press.

Children of the 90s. 2010. "Raves." *Children of the 90s*. Retrieved October 23, 2015 (http://childrenofthenineties.blogspot.com/2010/02/raves.html).

Clark, Fraser. 1992. "Shamanarchy." *Shamanarchy in The UK*. CD. London: Evolution Records.

Clarke, John, Stuart Hall, Tony Jefferson, and Brian Roberts. 1976. "Subcultures, Cultures, and Class." In *Resistance through Rituals: Youth Subcultures in Post-war Britain,* edited by Stuart Hall and Tony Jefferson, 9–74. New York: Routledge.

Cloud, John. 2001. "Ecstasy Crackdown. Will the Feds Use a 1980s Anti-Crack Law to Destroy the Rave Movement?" *Time Magazine,* April 9, 157 (13): 62–64.

Cloward, Richard A. and L.E. Ohlin. 1960. *Delinquency and Opportunity.* New York: Free Press.

Coates, Dennis and Brad R. Humphreys. 2008. "Do Economists Reach a Conclusion on Subsidies for Sports Franchises, Stadiums, and Mega-Events?" *Econ Journal Watch* 5 (3): 294–315.

Cohen, Albert K. 1955. *Delinquent Boys: The Culture of the Gang.* New York: The Free Press.

Cohen, Stanley. 1972. *Folk Devils and Moral Panics.* New York: Routledge.

Collin, Matthew. 2009. *Altered State: The Story of Ecstasy Culture and Acid House.* London: Serpent's Tail.

Conner, Christopher T. 2021. "How the Gay Party Scene Short-Circuited and became a Moneymaking Bonanza." *The Conversation,* February 12. Retrieved September 3, 2022 (https://theconversation.com/how-the-gay-party-scene-short-circuited-and -became-a-moneymaking-bonanza-153424).

Conner, Christopher T. and Daniel Okamura. 2021a. "Queer Expectations: An Empirical Critique of Rural LGBT+ Narratives." *Sexualities* (https://doi.org/10 .1177/13634607211013280).

Conner, Christopher T. and Daniel Okamura. 2021b. "Queering The Sociological Imagination." In *The Gayborhood From Sexual Liberation to Cosmopolitan Spectacle,* edited by C.T. Conner and D. Okamura, 1–14. Lanham, MD: Lexington Books.

Conner, Christopher T. and Nicholas MacMurray. 2021. "The Perfect Storm: A Subcultural Analysis of the QAnon Movement." *Critical Sociology* (https://doi.org /10.1177/08969205211055863).

Conner, Christopher T. and David R. Dickens. 2022. "Electric Empires: From Countercultural Movement to Corporate Enterprise." *Deviant Behavior* (https:// www.tandfonline.com/doi/full/10.1080/01639625.2022.2139208).

Conner, Christopher T. and Nathan Katz. 2020. "Electronic Dance Music: From Spectacular Subculture to Culture Industry." *Young: Nordic Journal of Youth Research* 28 (5): 445–464.

Cressey, Paul. 1932. *The Taxi-Dance Hall.* Chicago: University of Chicago Press.

Denzin, Norman K. 1994. "Postmodernism and Deconstructionism." In *Postmodernism and Social Inquiry,* edited by David R. Dickens and Andrea Fontana, 182–202. Lanham, MD: Guilford Press.

DJs from Mars. 2013. "Phat Ass Drop (How to Produce a Club Track)." Disco: wax.

Dickens, David R. 1994. "Cultural Studies in Sociology." *Symbolic Interaction* 17 (2): 99–105.

Domanick, Andrea. 2012. "Coachella Organizers Threatening to Take 2014 Off and Move the Festival Elsewhere." *LA Weekly,* July 3. Retrieved May 7, 2014. (http:// www.laweekly.com/westcoastsound/2012/07/03/coachella-organizers-threatening -to-take-2014-off-and- move-the-festival-elsewhere).

Dragonxninjaxpowa. 2008. "Why is Vinyl Better than Digital?" *Bluelight,* March 11. Retrieved October 23, 2015 (http://www.bluelight.org/vb/archive/index.php/t -396183-p- 3.html).

Drazen, Julie. 2004. *Rise: The Story of Rave Outlaw Disco Donnie*. Pottstown, PA: MVD Visual.

Durkheim, Emile. 1951 [1897]. *Suicide: A study in Sociology*. Translated by George Simpson. New York: The Free Press.

Eddy, Mark. 2003. "Ecstasy: Legislative Proposals in the 107th Congress to Control MDMA." *Congressional Research Service*. Retrieved October 21, 2015 (http://con gressionalresearch.com/RS21108/document.php?study=Ecstasy+Legislative+P roposals+in+the+107th+Congress+to+Control+MDMA).

EDM Sauce. 2014. "The Kinetic Cathedral: Largest Stage Ever Assembled in North America." *EDM Sauce,* June 23. Retrieved October 28, 2015 (http://www .edmsauce.com/2014/06/23/kinetic-cathedral-largest-stage-ever-assembled-north -america/).

EM:DEF. 2012. "Electronic Music Defense & Education Fund EMDEF." Accessed September 5, 2022 (https://web.archive.org/web/20120128131940/http://emdef .org/).

Eells, Josh. 2013. "Night Club Royale: Can Las Vegas Make More Money From Dance Music Than From Gambling?" *The New Yorker,* September 30. Retrieved October 22, 2015 (http://www.newyorker.com/magazine/2013/09/30/night-club -royale).

Epstein, Jonathon. 1994. *Adolescents and Their Music: If It's Too Loud, You're Too Old*. New York: Garland Publishing.

Feldberg, Sarah. 2011. "Las Vegas Has Become the EDM Capital of America." *Las Vegas Weekly,* June 2. Retrieved October 22, 2015 (http://lasvegasweekly.com/ news/2011/ jun/23/las-vegas-has-become-edm-capital-america-whats-nex/).

Fine, Gary A. and Sherryl Kleinman. 1979. "Rethinking Subculture: An Interactionist Analysis." *The American Journal of Sociology* 85 (1): 1–20.

Florida, Richard. 2003. *The Rise of the Creative Class: And How It's Transforming Work, Leisure, Community, and Everyday Life*. New York: Basic Books.

Fox, Kathryn Joan. 1987. "Real Punks and Pretenders: The Social Organization of a Counterculture." *Journal of Contemporary Ethnography* 16 (3): 344–370.

Frank, Thomas. 1997. *The Conquest of Cool*. Chicago: Chicago University Press.

Frazen, Benjamin and Kembrew McLeod. 2009. *Copyright Criminals*. DVD. New York: PBS.

Gelder, Ken. 2007. *Subcultures: Cultural Histories and Social Practice*. New York: Routledge.

Goode, Ebeneezer. 2004. *The Second Summer of Love*. DVD. London: BBC One.

Gottschalk, Simon. 1993. "Uncomfortably Numb: Countercultural Impulses in the Postmodern Era." *Symbolic Interaction* 16 (4): 351–378.

Haenfler, Ross. 2014. *Subcultures: The Basics*. New York: Routledge.

Haenfler, Ross. 2004. "Rethinking Subcultural Resistance: Core Values of the Straight Edge Movement." *Journal of Contemporary Ethnography* 33 (4): 406–436.

Haenfler, Ross, Brett Johnson, and Ellis Jones. 2012. "Lifestyle Movements: Exploring the Intersection of Lifestyle and Social Movements." *Social Movement Studies* 11 (1): 1–20.

Hebdige, Dick. 1979. *Subculture: The Meaning of Style*. New York: Routledge.

Herman, Sarah. 2012. "Hand in Glove: 'Gloving' Light Shows Dominate Raves, Stir Controversy." *LA Weekly,* June 28. Retrieved June 10, 2014 (http://www.laweekly.com/ 2012-06-28/music/gloving-raves-munch-lokey-emazing/).

Hidalgo, Danielle Antoinette. 2014. "Rave Culture." In *Encyclopedia of Social Deviance,* edited by Craig J. Forsyth and Heith Copes, 588–591. Thousand Oaks: Sage.

Hidalgo, Danielle Antoinette. 2022. *Dance Music Spaces: Clubs, Clubbers, and DJs Navigating Authenticity, Branding, and Commercialism.* Lanham, MD: Rowman and Littlefield.

Higgins, Will. 2013. "The Strange but True History of Indianapolis' Gay Bars." *Indianapolis Star,* December 12. Retrieved October 22, 2015 (http://www.indystar.com/story/life/2013/12/12/indianapolis-gay-bars/3997591/).

Hier, Sean P. 2002. "Raves, Risks and the Ecstacy Panic: A Case Study in the Subversive Nature of Moral Regulation." *The Canadian Journal of Sociology* 27 (1): 33–57.

Hill, Andrew. 2002. "Acid House and Thatcherism: Noise, the Mob, and the English Countryside." *British Journal of Sociology* 53 (1): 89–105.

Hindmarch, Carl. 2001. *Pump Up The Volume.* DVD. Chicago: Flame Television Ltd.

Hitzler, Ronald and Michaela Pfadenhauer. 2002. "Existential Strategies: The Making of Community and Politics in the Techno/Rave Scene." In *Postmodern Existential Sociology,* edited by Joseph A. Kotarba and John M. Johnson, 87–102. Lanham, MD: Rowman and Littlefield.

Hodkinson, Paul. 2002. *Goth: Identity, Style, and Subculture.* New York: Berg.

Horkheimer, Max and Theodor Adorno. 1972 [1944]. *Dialectic of Enlightenment.* Translated by John Cumming. New York: Continuum.

Hollywood, Brian. 1997. "Dancing in the Dark: Ecstasy, the Dance Culture, and Moral Panic in Post Ceasefire Northern Ireland." *Critical Criminology* 8 (1): 62–77.

Humphreys, Laud. 1972. *Out of the Closets: The Sociology of Homosexual Liberation.* Hoboken, NJ: Prentice Hall.

Irwin, John. 1977. *Scenes.* Thousand Oaks, CA: Sage.

Juzwiak, Rich. 2012. "Dance Dance Dissolution: The Electric Daisy Carnival's Fresh Hell." *Gawker,* May 30. Retrieved October 20, 2015 (http://gawker.com/5913180/dance-dance-dissolution-the-electric-daisy-carnivals-fresh-hell).

Katsilometes, John. 2013. "Pasquale Rotella's Taxing Statement: EDC's Return in 2014 in Jeopardy." *Las Vegas Sun,* April 25. Retrieved May 7, 2014. (http://www.lasvegassun.com/blogs/kats-report/2013/apr/25/rotellas-taxing-statement-edcs-return-2014-not-gua/).

Kellner, Douglas. 1989. *Critical Theory, Marxism, and Modernity.* Baltimore, MD: Johns Hopkins University Press.

Kellner, Douglas. 2003. *Media Spectacle.* New York: Routledge.

Kelley, Thomas. 2014. "10 Things: New-School Ravers vs. Old-School Ravers." *Insomniac,* June 11. Retrieved November 8, 2015 (https://www.insomniac.com/media/10-things-new-school-ravers-vs-old-school-ravers).

Kitsuse, John I. 1975. "The New Conception of Deviance and Its Critics." In *The Labeling of Deviance: Evaluating a Perspective,* edited by W. Grove, 273–283. New York: Sage.

Komenda, Ed. 2013. "Raising the Bar: Five-story, $100 million Hakkasan Setting a Precedent for Las Vegas Nightlife." *Las Vegas Sun*, April 18. Retrieved September 3, 2022 (https://vegasinc.lasvegassun.com/business/2013/apr/18/five-story-100 -million-hakkasan-sets-precedent-las/).

Kosmicki, Guillaume. 2001. "Musical Meaning in Today's Free-Parties: Between Ideology and Utopia." *Societes* 2 (1): 35–44.

Lawrence, Tim. 2016. "Life and Death on the Pulse Dance Floor: Transglocal Politics and the Erasure of the Latinx in the History of Queer Dance." *Dancecult* 8 (1): 1–25.

Liazos, Alexander. 1972. "The Poverty of the Sociology of Deviance: Nuts, Sluts, and Perverts." *Social Problems* 20 (1): 103–120.

Little, Noah. 2018. "EDM and Ecstasy: The Lived Experiences of Electronic Dance Music Festival Attendees." *Journal of New Music Research* 47 (1): 78–95.

Lloyd, Richard. 2006. *Neo-Bohemia: Art and Commerce in the Postindustrial City*. New York: Routledge.

Lofland, Lyn H. 1998. *The Public Realm: Quintessential City Life*. Piscataway, NJ: Aldine de Gruyter.

Liu, Le Shing. 2019. *The Last Dance* (https://www.amazon.com/Last-Dance-Liu/dp /B07NJ2RKLT).

Madden, David. 2016. "DJ Mini and Montreal's Vulgar Dance Music." *Dancecult: Journal of Electronic Dance Music Culture* 8 (1): 26–45.

Maffesoli, Michel. 1996. *The Time of the Tribes: The Decline of Individualism in Mass Society*. London: Sage.

Marcuse, Herbert. 1964. *One-Dimensional Man: Studies in the Ideology of Advanced IndustrialSociety*. Boston: Beacon

Marcuse, Herbert. 1968 [1937]. "The Affirmative Character of Culture." In *Negations: Essays in Critical Theory,* translated by Jeremy Shapiro, 88–133. Boston: Beacon Press.

Matos, Michaelangelo. 2011. "How the Internet Transformed the American Rave Scene." *NPR*, July 11. Retrieved October 22, 2015 (http://www.npr.org/sections/ therecord/2011/07/17/137680680/how-the-internet-transformed-the-american-rave -scene).

Matos, Michaelangelo. 2015. *The Underground Is Massive: How Electronic Dance Music Conquered America*. New York: Harper Collins.

Malbon, Ben. 1999. *Clubbing: Dancing, Ecstasy, and Vitality*. New York: Routledge.

Masquelier, Charles. 2013. "Critical Theory and Contemporary Social Movements: Conceptualizing Resistance in the Neoliberal Age." *European Journal of Social Theory* 16 (4): 395–412.

McCall, Tara. 2001. *This is Not a Rave: In the Shadow of a Subculture*. New York: Thunder's Mouth Press.

McGuigan, Jim. 1992. *Cultural Populism*. New York: Routledge.

McLeod, Kembrew and Peter DiCola. 2011. *Creative License: The Law and Culture of Digital Sampling*. Durham, NC: Duke University Press.

McRobbie, Angela. 1994. *Postmodernism and Popular Culture*. New York, NY: Routledge.

Mears, Ashley. 2020. *Very Important People: Status and Beauty in the Global Party Circuit*. Princeton, NJ: Princeton University Press.

Merton, Robert K. 1949. *Social Theory and Social Structure*. New York: The Free Press.

Mills, C. Wright. 1943. "The Professional Ideology of Social Pathologists." *American Journal of Sociology* 49 (2): 165–180.

Motl, Kaitlyne A. 2018. "Dashiki Chic: Color-blind Racial Ideology in EDM Festivalgoers' "Dress Talk."" *Popular Music and Society* 41 (3): 250–269.

Muggelton, David. 2000. *Inside Subculture: The Postmodern Meaning of Style*. New York: Berg.

Munzenrieder, Kyle. 2013. "Why The Corporate Takeover of EDM Was Inevitable: The Straight Bros Are on Board." *The Miami New Times,* March 15. Retrieved October 22, 2015 (http://www.miaminewtimes.com/news/why-the-corporate-take-over-of-edm-was-inevitable-the-straight-bros-are-on-board-6546280).

Murji, Karim. 1998. "The Agony and the Ecstasy: Drugs, Media and Morality." In *The Control of Drugs and Drug Users: Reason of Reaction,* edited by Ross Coomber, 46–53. Amsterdam: Harwood Academic Publishers.

Ott, Brian L. and Bill D. Herman. 2003. "Mixed Messages: Resistance and Reappropriation in Rave Culture." *Western Journal of Communication* 67 (3): 249–270.

Owen, Frank. 2003. *Clubland: The Fabulous Rise and Murderous Rise of Club Culture*. New York: St. Martin's Press.

Palmer, Vivien M. 1928. *Field Studies in Sociology: A Student's Manual*. Chicago: University of Chicago Press.

Panfil, Vanessa. 2017. *The Gang's All Queer*. New York, NY: NYU Press.

Park, Robert E., Ernest W. Burgess, and Roderick D. McKenzie. 1925. *The City*. Chicago: University of Chicago Press.

Park, Judy Soojin. 2015. "Searching for a Cultural Home: Asian American Youth in the EDM Festival Scene." *Dancecult* 7 (1): 15–34.

Peretti, Jacques. 2006. "History in the Remaking." *The Guardian*, June 10. Retrieved May 5, 2014 (http://www.theguardian.com/media/2006/jun/10/tvandradio.theguide).

Piccone, Paul. 1978. "The Crisis of One-Dimensionality." *Telos* 35 (1): 43–54.

Plummer, K. 2011. "The Labelling Perspective Forty Years On." In *Langweiliges Verbrechen. VS Verlag für Sozialwissenschaften*, edited by H. Peters and M. Dellwing. https://doi.org/10.1007/978-3-531-93402-0_5.

Polsky, Ned. 1967. *Hustlers, Beats, and Others*. New York, NY: Routledge.

Powell, Nicole. 2012. "Electric Daisy Carnival Brings $207 Million to Las Vegas' Local Economy." *Hollywood Reporter*, October 2. Retrieved November 23, 2015 (http://www. hollywoodreporter.com/earshot/electric-daisy-canival-las-vegas-ec onomy-207-375901).

Pratt, Jane. 1992. "The Jane Pratt Show." *Lifetime Network*. Retrieved September 6, 2022 (https://www.youtube.com/watch?v=OG5D_SBTbds).

Prevatt, Mike. 2014. "Report: EDC 2014 Brought in $338 Million for The Las Vegas Valley." *Las Vegas Weekly,* November 14. Retrieved June 20, 2015 (http://lasvegasweekly.com/nightlife/2014/nov/14/edc-electronic-daisy-carnival -2014- economic-impact/).

Ramos, Josell. 2003. *Maestro*. DVD. New York: Artution Productions.

Rappaport, Jill. 1992. "Raving." *The Today Show.* Retrieved September 6, 2022 (https://www.youtube.com/watch?v=3xCljwXTntY).

Redhead, Steve. 1993. *Rave Off: Politics and Deviance in Contemporary Youth Culture.* Brookfield, VT: Avebury.

Reynolds, Simon. 1999. *Generation Ecstasy: Into the World of Techno and Rave Culture.* New York: Routledge.

Reynolds, Simon. 2012. "How Rave Music Conquered America." *The Guardian,* August 2. Retrieved October 22, 2015 (http://www.theguardian.com/music/2012/ aug/02/how-rave-music-conquered-america).

Rilling, Deanna. 2008. "Saturdays, Perfecto'd." *Las Vegas Sun,* August 28. Retrieved October 22, 2015 (http://lasvegassun.com/news/2008/aug/28/saturdays -perfectod/).

Romero, Dennis. 2011. "Raves Might be Reined in Under Fiona Ma's Bill, Which Just passed The California Legislature." *LA Weekly Blogs,* September 9. Retrieved July 10, 2014 (http://www.laweekly.com/informer/2011/09/09/raves-might-be -reined-in-unde-fiona-mas-bill-which-just-passed-the-california-legislature).

Rosenbaum, Marsha. 2002. "Ecstasy: America's New Reefer Madness." *Journal of Psychoactive Drugs* 34 (2): 137–142.

Ross, Christopher. 2015. "Q&As With Afrojack, Avicii and David Guetta." *Wallstreet Journal,* April 2. Retrieved October 22, 2015 (http://www.wsj.com/ articles/q-as-with-afrojack-avicii-and-david-guetta-1427993631).

Rothstein, Richard. 2017. *The Color of Law: A Forgotten History of How our Government Segregated America.* New York, NY: Liveright Publishing Corporation.

Rotella, Pasquale. 2013. "An Important Message From Pasquale To You." *Insomniac,* June 19. Retrieved October 22, 2015 (https://web.archive.org/web /20130625010216/ http://insomniac.com/newsDetails.php?news=503).

Rushkoff, Douglas. 1994. *Cyberia: Life in the Trenches of Cyberspace.* New York, NY: Clinamen Press Ltd..

Sager, Rebekah. 2012. "Madonna Takes Ultra to the Next Level, References Ecstasy Use." *Fox News Latino,* March 26. Retrieved October 22, 2015 (http://latino .foxnews.com/latino/entertainment/2012/03/26/madonna-takes-ultra-to-next-level -references-ecstasy-use/).

Saraceno, C.J. 2013. "Electric Zoo: A Manifestation of the East Coast Version of EDM." *CJ Saraceno,* September 1. Retrieved October 22, 2015 (http://cjsaraceno .com/tag/electric- zoo/).

Schlemback, Raphael. 2015. "Negation, Refusal and Co-Optation: The Frankfurt School and Social Movement Theory." *Sociology Compass* 9 (11): 987–999.

Scott, Michael S., ed. 2002. *Rave Parties. Problem-Oriented Guides for Police Series* No. 14. Washington DC: United States Department of Justice. Retrieved June 10, 2013. (http://www.cops. usdoj.gov/pdf/e12011406.pdf).

Sein, Christina L. 2004. "The Agony and the Ecstasy: Preserving First Amendment Freedoms in the Government's War on Raves." *Southern California Interdisciplinary Law Journal* 12 (139): 139–165.

Shah, Neil. 2015. "How Music Festivals Pump Billions into the U.S. Economy." *Wallstreet Journal*, July 31. Retrieved November 20, 2015 (http://blogs.wsj.com/speakeasy/ 2015/07/31/how-music-festivals-pump-billions-into-the-u-s-economy/).

Shaw, Clifford R. 1930. *The Jack-Roller*. Chicago: University of Chicago Press.

Silcott, Mireille. 1999. *Rave America*. Chicago: ECW Press.

Siokou, Christine and David Moore. 2008. "This is not a Rave! Changes in the Commercialized Melbourne Rave/Dance Party Scene." *Youth Studies Australia* 27 (3): 50–57.

St. John, Graham, eds. 2004. *Rave Culture and Religion*. New York: Routledge.

St. John, Graham, eds. 2009. *Technomad: Global Raving Counterculture*. Oakville, CT: Equinox Publishing.

Strong, Ronald L. 2001. "National Drug Intelligence Center: Assessing the Drug Threat." *Police Chief* 68 (5): 55–60.

Sutherland, Edwin. 1937. *The Professional Thief*. Chicago: University of Chicago Press.

Test, Irene. 2012. "Why EDM Isn't Fully Accepted." *Crossfadr,* October 7. Retrieved October 22, 2015 (http://www.crossfadr.com/2012/10/07/why-edm-isnt -fully-accepted/).

Thomas, Anthony. 1995. "The House the Kids Built: The Gay Black Imprint on American Dance Music." In *Out in Culture*, edited by Corey K. Creelmun and Alexander Doty, 437–445. Durham, NC: Duke University Press.

Thomas, W.I. and Florian Znaniecki. 1918. *The Polish Peasant in Europe and America*. Chicago: University of Chicago Press.

Thornton, Sarah. 1996. *Club Cultures: Music, Media, and Subcultural Capital*. Middletown: Wesleyan.

Tullberg, Michael. 2014. *Dancefloor Thunderstorm: Land of the Free, Home of the Rave*. Los Angeles, CA: 5150 Publishing.

Turner, Graeme. 1990. *British Cultural Studies*. New York: Routledge.

Victor, Jeffrey S. 1993. *Satanic Panic: The Creation of a Contemporary Legend*. Chicago, IL: Open Court.

Vitos, Botond. 2017. "The Dance Floor Experiment: Researching the Mediating Technologies and Embodied Experiences of Electronic Dance Music Events." *Popular Music and Society* 40 (2): 131–150.

Weber, Marx. 1930 [1905]. *The Protestant Ethic and the Sprit of Captialism*. Thousand Oaks: Routledge.

Weems, Mickey. 2008. *The Fierce Tribe: Masculine Identity and Performance in the Circuit*. St. Lake City: Utah State University Press.

Weir, Erica. 2000. "Raves: A Review of the Culture, the Drugs and the Prevention of Harm." *Canadian Medical Association Journal* 162 (13): 1843–1848.

Wender, Dan. 2015. "How Frankie Bones' Storm Rave Birthed the PLUR Movement." *Thump,* May 13. Retrieved November 7, 2015 (https://thump.vice.com/en_us/article/how-frankie- bones-storm-rave-birthed-the-plur-movement).

Weinstein, Steve. 2014. "Dance Music Is My Religion: Steve Weinstein on the Sacred Origins of Gay Circuit Parties." *Vice News*, December 15. Retrieved September 3, 2022 (https://www.vice.com/en/article/d7eb3m/dance-music-is-my-religion-steve -weinstein-on-the-sacred-origins-of-gay-circuit-parties).

Williams, J. Patrick. 2011. *Subcultural Theory: Traditions and Concepts*. Malden: Polity.

Willis, Paul. 1977. *Learning to Labor: How Working Class Kids Get Working Class Jobs*. New York: Columbia University Press.

Wilson, Brian. 2006. *Fight, Flight, or Chill: Subculture, Youth, and Rave into the Twenty-First Century*. Montreal: McGill-Queen's University Press.

Wiltsher, Nick. 2016. "The Aesthetics of Electronic dance Music, Part 1: History, Genre, Scenes, Identity, Blackness." *Philosophy Copmass* 11 (8): 415–425.

Winterbottom, Michael. 2002. *24 Hour Party People*. DVD. Los Angeles: Revolution Films.

Yocoubian, George S. Jr., Sarah Miller, Selwyn Pianim, Michael Kunz, Erin Orrick, Tanja Link, Wilson R. Palacios, and Ronald J. Peters. 2004. "Toward an Ecstasy and Other Club Drug (EOCD) Prevention Intervention for Rave Attendees." *Journal of Drug Education* 34 (1): 41–59.

Yacoubian, George S. Jr. and Eric D. Wish. 2006. "Exploring the Validity of Self-Reported Ecstasy Use among Club Rave Attendees." *Journal of Psychoactive Drugs* 38 (1): 31–34.

Yinger, Milton J. 1960. "Contraculture and Subculture." *American Sociological Review* 25 (5): 625–635.

Zimmerman, Joel. 2012. "We All Hit Play." *Tumblr*. Retrieved October 22, 2015 (http://deadmau5.tumblr.com/post/25690507284/we-all-hit-play).

Zizek, Slavoj. 1997. "Multiculturalism, or, The Cultural Logic of Multinational Capitalism." *New Left Review* 1 (225): 28–51.

Index

Note: Page numbers in *italics* denotes figures.

About the Authors

Christopher T. Conner is non-tenure track teaching assistant professor of sociology at The University of Missouri, Columbia. His research is at the intersection of criminology/deviance, social movements, technology, gender and sexuality, and social theory. His work explores how subgroups become legitimate in the mind of the public and how these groups maintain their autonomy and commitment to core values in light of these shifts. He has explored this process for members of the Electronic Dance Music Subculture, Gay Men and Gay Spaces, and how right-wing extremists exploit this achieve legitimacy within contemporary politics. He has also co-edited numerous anthologies including *The Gayborhood: From Sexual Liberation to Cosmopolitan Spectacle*, *Forgotten Founders and Other Neglected Social Theorists*, and *Studies in Symbolic Interaction: Subcultures*. He is series editor for *The Frankfurt School in New Times* book series at Lexington Books and is currently editing a volume on extremist movements and conspiracy theories for Lexington Books.

David R. Dickens was professor of sociology at the University of Nevada, Las Vegas. He published extensively on social theory, community, leisure and identity, and culture. Additionally, his work included studies on the culture of Iran. His work explores how individuals react to larger historical and structural changes happening in society. His 41 publications include an edited volume titled *Postmodernism and Social Inquiry* with Andrea Fontana and *Las Vegas: The Social Production of an All-American City*. He was co-editor of *Neglected Theorists of Color* from Lexington Books with Korey Tillman and Chico Herbison.

www.ingramcontent.com/pod-product-compliance
Lightning Source LLC
Chambersburg PA
CBHW031138270326
41929CB00011B/1670